YOU CAN'T DO IT ALONE

YOU CAN'T DO IT ALONE

FOCUSING ON PEOPLE TO SCALE, DEVELOP, AND LEAD YOUR RESTAURANT

MATT ROLFE

LIONCREST
PUBLISHING

YOU CAN'T DO IT ALONE
Focusing on People to Scale, Develop, and Lead Your Restaurant

ISBN   978-1-5445-2048-3 *Hardcover*
      978-1-5445-2047-6 *Paperback*
      978-1-5445-2046-9 *Ebook*

In support of this book, we have created Westshore Online. In our three-hour, fully interactive Executive Leadership Mastery program, we dive deeper into the topics covered in each chapter of this book. We invite you to continue the learning experience online, where you will have access to not only the digital versions of worksheets from the book but many more!

Visit us at **mattrolfe.com** for the next piece of the leadership puzzle.

This is dedicated to all the teachers who
told me I would never amount to nothin'...
—Notorious BIG

First off, I want to thank our industry for accepting me, developing me, and providing me the opportunity to do what I love every day.

To James and the team, this is not my book; this is our book. It is a collection of our combined experiences over the last fifteen years. To look at where we started, the fun we had, the challenges we overcame, and where we are now puts a smile on my face...and we're only getting started.

One of my goals in life was to find ways to say thank you to my mom and my dad for everything they did for me growing up. Even with everything we went through, I would not change a thing, and although you're not here with me, I hope this makes you proud.

Lindsay, you are my source of love, inspiration, and motivation. There is no one in this world who inspires me more than you do on a daily basis, and your belief in me and continued support are the drive behind this book. Thank you!

Kenzie, my goal as a father is to do my best to lead by example, to never limit our opportunities, and to be present and have fun along the way. You are my world, kiddo.

CONTENTS

FOREWORD

by Devin Hastie, Director of Commercial Learning,
Anheuser-Busch North America

Have you ever met someone for the first time, and in that moment, you think "I'm pretty sure I hate this guy"? You don't know why, but there is just something you can't put a finger on. Something familiar.

The hospitality industry is all about first impressions, but this is a story of lasting impressions.

I would consider Matt Rolfe one of a few close friends and a confidant within an industry that is changing faster than some people change their underwear. But as already established, we weren't always friends. We first met over twenty years ago in the rum aisle in a government liquor store in Creemore, Ontario. A fitting place, where our small-town values were starting to evolve into big-city dreams. Matt was working for Bacardi, and I was making a sales call for a large beer company.

My first impression of Matt was that I didn't like him. He was forward, passionate, articulate, and assertive. He was a threat to my aspirations because he was more competent than the other salespeople I had to compete with at that time. As I reflect back, I realized it was only because Matt was just like me, minus the articulate piece. When you see those qualities in a competitor, even if it's not a direct competitor, it makes you feel defensive and threatened.

We started to cross paths more frequently and were even spending time together at professional functions. Watching Matt interact with people in this environment, it became obvious that he was a young, motivated individual who was mature beyond his years. He was passionate, curious, and innovative and had the ability to build authentic relationships. Instead of continuing to feel that "I don't like this guy," my impression of Matt changed drastically and my thoughts changed to, "How do we get this guy on our team?"

Matt has unique expertise in connecting multiple complex, moving pieces. He's able to bring the power of authentic leadership to the areas that drive business, whether it's first-class service, operational efficiency, or profitability. He understands leadership requires effort and purpose.

I'm not surprised that all these years later, Matt is revered as a leader within the food and beverage industry. He's a chameleon who can adapt to most if not all situations, social and business-related. He also has an innate ability to know when people are not being straight with him. Matt is able to ask uncomfortable questions people might not be ready to face in a way that allows them to face the reality and truth in a safe environment. Those abilities, along with his diverse experiences working on both the operations and supplier side of the industry, separate him from most other experts.

The world is getting more complex, and the food and beverage industry is changing faster than ever. What used to be successful twenty years, months, or weeks ago is not necessarily successful today. In order to cope, operators need help, inspiration, and provocation to think differently so they don't get stuck in the habits that prevent them from moving their business forward. That's why my organization, one of the biggest beer companies in the world, chose to work with Matt and Westshore Hospitality Group when we realized we needed help understanding the challenges our own customers were facing.

This book will provoke leaders to think about how to adapt to a changing environment, how to be honest with themselves, and how to challenge themselves. Through Matt's experience and wisdom and the examples of real-life operators, this book will take you and your company from the insanity of doing the same thing over and over again and expecting different results to awareness that hopefully ends in growth. It will help you unleash potential and effect the positive change needed to survive in a fast-changing industry.

As I age (let's call it mature; I hate to think I am getting old) and authentic relationships become even more important to me, I sure am thankful that first impressions don't always supersede lasting impressions.

INTRODUCTION

"Our intention creates our reality."

—Wayne Dyer

Let me show you what crisis looks like.

I met Clark Lishman in the summer of 2017 to talk about Turtle Jack's. Turtle Jack's is one of the largest restaurant groups I coach; they have outlets all over Ontario, Canada. Clark was the son of the owner—this young, successful entrepreneur poised to take over his dad's company. He understood that there had been incredible success in the business to get it where it was, but he also understood that, simply based on changes in the industry and how businesses now operate, Turtle Jack's was going to have to evolve. That's why he got in touch with me; he wanted to change the direction of the business.

In our first few meetings, Clark repeated one thing over and over, *What can I do for my team and my people?*

Our first face-to-face meeting was in his office. I drove down from my office in Toronto to the suburbs and pulled up in front of this beautiful building. Clark's Porsche, bearing his signature license plates, was parked out front; I tapped it lightly on my way through the double doors. I went up the elevators and into this beautiful office—wood-paneled, with this finely crafted desk in the middle. And on the other side of the desk was Clark.

Throughout that meeting, Clark was incredible. He was engaging, a great speaker, and he knew his business inside out. As he talked, I sat opposite him and tried to get a feel for where he was emotionally at. And the more he talked, the more I realized we were deflecting. Clark wanted to know what we could do for his team and his people. But what we really needed to talk about was him.

Throughout this, Clark's phone and computer were lighting up. I could see Clark consistently glancing at his phone as the messages poured in. I could see his eyes flit to his computer screen each time an email slid in or an appointment popped up. For 30 minutes into that meeting, the notifications didn't stop. And so, at the 30-minute mark, I asked him to turn his monitor around so that I could see it. And then I said, *Show me your calendar.*

Clark pulled up his calendar, and his body language...shifted. His shoulders sank. He slid down slightly in that office chair. He glanced at his knees, quickly, involuntarily—and when he looked up, tears were rolling down his face.

The reason is because that calendar was a representation of everything expected of Clark. The hours, the capacity, the decision-making. And it wasn't sustainable. For the average person, it wasn't even possible. And yet this was Clark's expectation and reality every single day. It was crushing him personally.

I changed the direction of the meeting in that moment. We talked about where that weight and emotion was coming from. We realized all these messages and work pressure was separating Clark from his family. All his energy was directed toward work. And no matter how hard Clark worked, at the end of the day, there would still be a mountain left to climb.

Clark's story is your story. It's the story of so many leaders I've worked with over the years. We think we have to do it alone. Doing it alone means working it around the clock. Doing it alone means being responsible for making every decision or being *part* of making every decision in your organization. Doing it alone means micromanaging your team when you don't want to and your people hate it.

And the risk of that is your business won't grow. It cannot. You will burn out. Your people will quit and leave. What people want in their employment after their base financial needs are met is growth and development. If you're not providing that, they will leave you. There's no way to scale a business without a foundation of *development* within your own organization. You *cannot* grow a multiscale restaurant group by simply continuously recruiting from the outside and keeping all the responsibility with you.

You cannot do it alone.

You probably know this. Some part of you has sensed that this way of working isn't sustainable. But if you're a top-performing restaurant operator, then you're always looking to expand your business—you want to get to the next level. You even know what that level looks like. But the challenge is *reaching* that level. The more you try, the more difficult it gets. You're at capacity. You can't fit anything more into your weeks, personally or professionally.

And the more the business expands, the more you move away from the things you loved about your profession.

I was working with a multisite restaurant group in one of the highest tourist-traffic areas in Toronto. I was coaching the executive vice president, Tim—an incredible leader—and I loved working with the guy. But Tim always had a block. And when I asked him what that resistance was, he said, *Matt, I spend my entire days on email. I got into this business as a chef, and it's been months since I touched or interacted with food.*

That distance wears you down. Tim couldn't muster more energy for what he was doing because he couldn't do what he loved—what got him *into* the business in the first place. Instead, he was buried under a mountain of things he didn't love doing and that never seemed to get done.

To make matters worse, dealing with the pandemic presented new challenges for all of us to face. Maybe you dealt with staffing problems—because let's be honest: who didn't? After all, the average bar/restaurant experiences 100 percent turnover *every year*.

Or maybe you're looking for consistency when increasing the number of locations. This was Layne Krienke's greatest fear about doubling the number of restaurants for the JOEY Restaurant Group. The JOEY Restaurant Group is one of North America's most successful restaurant groups—it had twenty-plus locations when I started working with them. Layne was their incoming president. And his fear as they began opening more restaurants was, *Do we have the people to execute consistency?* He understood that if they didn't deliver consistent experiences—for their guests, their people, and in terms of quality of food and drink—then their concept would fail. The key to successfully scaling any restaurant group is always consistency; without it, your growth will bottleneck. Or worse, implode.

Or maybe you've snagged the top-rated server or bartender in the entire city, but you find they don't share your values. If that's the case, then I don't give a shit if they're the best. If they don't believe in the experience you're creating for guests or how you communicate with your team, they don't fit your culture. They need to go. Now. They will fill their pockets full of money and tips, and they will leave a gaping hole in your team once they leave or a gaping hole in your culture in the day-to-day of how your operation runs.

Whether you own and operate a handful of restaurants or you're in charge of a restaurant group representing hundreds of locations, one thing is certain: you can't do it alone. What got you to where you are today will *not* get you to where you want to go, which is why you picked up this book.

The fact that you're reading this tells me you're not only gutsy, determined, and creative but also smart and savvy. You're looking to make your business even *more* successful than it already is, and this book will lay out the formula to help you get there.

But simply reading a book will not get you there. You have to put in the work.

DON'T JUST CONSUME CONTENT

There's certainly no shortage of information on how to improve, how to grow, or how to find even more success, but all that information is useless unless we act. We've become addicted to consuming content, but then we get stuck when it comes to actually applying what we've learned.

And the worldwide pandemic of 2020 didn't make things any easier, either.

In fact, it only brought on more challenges—and I'm not talking about uphill struggles in navigating the ever-changing rules imposed by the shutdown. As we spent more time in our homes social distancing, we consumed even more content—content that just went in one ear and out the other.

This book is no different. I can't emphasize enough how important it is for you to *apply* what you read in the pages that follow. One of the exercises I do in my workshops is called the spin cycle. It's a diagram of a funnel broken down into four sections. The top of the funnel—the widest mouth—is awareness. The section below that is choice. The next one is decision. And then out of the funnel comes action. The purpose of a funnel is to put *downward* pressure to force a result. But that rarely happens. What happens instead is that top-performing operators have more choice than they can wrap their arms around. So they spin continuously between awareness and choice. You'll see it in the diagram; it's a cycle. Almost all the operators I ask feel like they're only getting 80 percent of things done and they can't get to 100 percent—things aren't getting completed. They're just lost in opportunity. That's because they're not putting any downward pressure on the funnel; they've lost their intention. They never move from choice to decision, and so they never see any action or results. They just spin, and spin, and spin, with 80 percent to 90 percent of projects completed but none to the level they want or deserve. It creates friction, tension, and stress for *everybody* in the organization.

What I'm going to teach you in this book is how to get all the way through the funnel. I'm going to show you how to create

SPIN CYCLE DYNAMIC

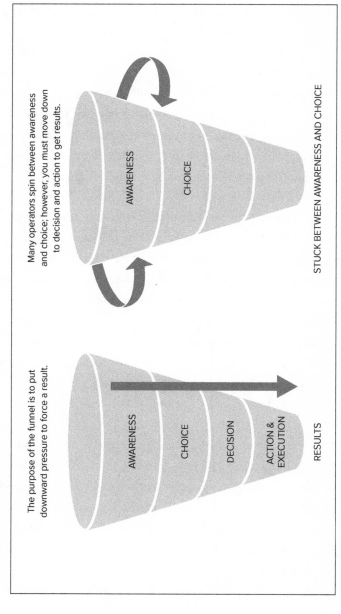

The purpose of the funnel is to put downward pressure to force a result.

AWARENESS

CHOICE

DECISION

ACTION & EXECUTION

RESULTS

Many operators spin between awareness and choice; however, you must move down to decision and action to get results.

AWARENESS

CHOICE

STUCK BETWEEN AWARENESS AND CHOICE

MATT ROLFE

WESTSHORE ONLINE

mattrolfe.com

intention so that you move from choice to decision and then to clear *action*, so that your organization sees results.

But to do that effectively, your team has to be involved in your execution strategy. Owners and senior leaders often start out by doing everything themselves until their business outgrows this approach. Unfortunately, many leaders don't recognize this moment and they themselves become the limiting factor in their company's own growth because they keep doing what they've always done. They often hold on to too much of the decision-making, so when everyone is coming to you for guidance or approval on every little thing, you're hindering your own forward progress— not to mention how incredibly frustrating this is on both sides.

We have to get out of our own way in order to step forward as the leader that our business needs us to be. That starts with building a solid team and delegating tasks off of our plates. You can't do it alone! Your team members need to be leaders—not just doers—capable of coaching and mentoring staff. Where processes, clear expectations, coaching, and recognition might not have formally been needed in the past, they certainly will be necessary moving forward to ensure the day-to-day business runs the way they want it to.

This people part of the business trips us up. Things like leadership, communication, hiring, training, and retention are all *learned* skills. Many busy owners feel they don't have the time or expertise to acquire these skills, but the only way to have a thriving, sustainable, scalable business is to attract, retain, and engage people who believe what you believe and help to build momentum behind your vision.

So, learn you must. Luckily, you're in the right place to do just that.

MY BACKGROUND

Through my consulting firm, Westshore Hospitality Group, I coach the top 10 percent of industry operators with the highest-volume, top-performing, fastest-growing operations in North America. Together, we come up with people-based solutions to make their businesses even stronger and more profitable. I've written this book to teach you the same strategies I use with my clients to help you achieve the next stage of growth and opportunity for your business.

Back in school, my teachers probably didn't think I'd be able to lay claim to all that. In fact, they pretty much told me I'd never be a success at anything. Diagnosed with a learning disability early on in life, I repeated first grade twice, skipped third, and then got placed in "learning strategies" classes for the rest of my elementary and high school education.

Teachers had very low expectations for me, and I was always fighting the system. I was often told I would never accomplish anything. In fact, some even said I lacked the cognitive ability to graduate high school, and I should plan to look for alternative routes of employment. *Fuck that*, I told myself. *I'll show them.* All of the doubt and negativity motivated me to graduate high school and go to college—and I did.

When I found my way into hospitality during college, I instantly fell in love with the industry and its people. My experience with them was utterly refreshing—they were willing to accept me regardless of how I had performed in school. They accepted me and didn't judge or underestimate me like my teachers had. They didn't care about my transcripts. They cared about what I brought to the table. Because I could sell and communicate well, they were willing to invest in me, help me develop, and give me opportunities to grow.

One of my earliest experiences was with Labatt Breweries—now owned by Anheuser-Busch breweries—which was such a fun job. But what baffled me and blew my mind was finding out the successful-looking guys I was selling to only *looked* successful on the outside. In reality, their businesses were not profitable. In fact, they were hemorrhaging money. They were among the top ten sellers of my beer, but they were basically broke.

After witnessing one too many owners in tears over the state of their finances, I became passionate about helping operators change this trend. I joined a firm focused on enhancing profits for bar restaurants—and we kicked ass. My team could go into any place in North America and, in the first twelve months, find a way to add a hundred thousand dollars to their bottom line.

In taking restaurant groups through the steps that lead to a more profitable business, I discovered that success didn't come from the consulting process—it came from human connection and behavior change. This is consistent across all industries, whether it be retail, insurance, or hospitality.

Throughout my twenty years in the hospitality industry, I've helped hundreds of top-performing, multisite, high-revenue independent restaurants elevate their businesses and find momentum. I've helped countless leaders establish a foundation to maximize efficiencies in their staff, which improved morale and significantly decreased turnover. Change isn't easy, but the results are always worth it.

Although my passion is helping those who are open to change, I can't want it more for you than you want it for yourself. Facilitating change and building a successful restaurant is no accident. It's intentional, and it requires commitment. If you're ready to begin thinking differently about your operation, solidify the direction you want to go, and execute strategy, then this book will be a tremendous help to you.

Over the past fifteen years with Westshore Hospitality Group, we have studied hundreds of operations and identified what the top 10 percent do fundamentally differently from the rest of the industry. What do they do that makes them stand out from the competition? You'll find the answers and how you can also land among the top 10 percent in the pages that follow. The concepts within aren't merely ideas, either—they have been studied, implemented, and put into practice. They've been tested, challenged, proven, and improved. Everything presented to you in this book is based on experience, successes, and failures.

TAKE YOUR BUSINESS TO THE NEXT LEVEL

We all know the restaurant business is tough. Eighty percent of restaurants go bankrupt within three to five years. An average restaurant in North America experiences profitability at less than 5 percent. Most restaurants experience significantly higher than 100 percent annual staff turnover. And thanks to COVID, 50 percent of restaurants are expected to close or not reopen. Of those that are surviving and running, over 65 percent are currently losing money and 19 percent are at breakeven.

Add to that the long hours and the many hats you wear, and you can see how everything takes a toll on you and your restaurant or restaurant group. The challenges *really* start pouring in when restaurants grow quickly and owners can't find a way to delegate properly to their management team and staff. Owners then become stressed out and overworked, and as a result, they can't be effective leaders. This stress then leads to a lack of communication, which then leads to turnover, costing the business a ton of money.

If that sounds like you and you're not getting the revenue, profitability, or scalability you deserve from your restaurant, it's time to try something new. As the saying goes, insanity is doing the same thing over and over again and expecting a different result.

You picked this book up because something is harder than it needs to be. You might not even be able to put it into words, but you're frustrated and you want to reach the next level. But in order for you to do that, something's got to change—and it starts with you.

You don't need to be the smartest person in the room to make it in this business—just ask my teachers.

And you don't have to work *harder* either.

You just have to be willing to change your mindset—and help the people in your organization do the same.

All the strategies in this book have been implemented by top-performing restaurant groups. They got great results, and so will you. In the chapters that follow, you'll learn how to:

- Lead with vulnerability and authenticity
- Define—with laser focus—your one- and three-year strategies
- Communicate your vision with your team, and get them to buy into and implement it consistently
- Co-create with and invest in your staff, getting their feedback and allowing people to spend time on the things that truly move the business forward to achieve its goals

- Communicate with your team consistently and effectively to create positive leverage
- Execute a 100-day plan at your business

I've divided the chapters in this book by topic. There are dozens of useful lessons throughout these pages, but I encourage you to be selfish and selective. Look at the table of contents, find the topic that will have the biggest impact for you, and start there. Cameron Herold, author of *Double Double*, says he wants his readers to go to the chapter they need. Understand the concept of the book, sure, but go to what you need to read the most. Find the one topic that would have the biggest impact on your growth, team, and business today and start your journey there.

If you're reading this book in order, then here's how it's set out. I'll talk you through high-level concepts first. A lot of what you need to do as a top-performing operator and owner is change who you become and how you *approach* things. These are mindset shifts that will have powerful ripples on your organization. From there, we'll move down to the more tactical chapters, like a waterfall. As you know from this Introduction, we're dedicated to making sure you can *act* on the ideas in this book, so I promise you that by the end of the last chapter, you will have enough effective execution strategies and actionable steps toward your goals—as well as a 100-day plan to help you get there.

As an entrepreneur who has tried and failed more than most, my goal is to provide you with insight from my experiences into proven approaches that can help you run a better business. When leaders and leadership teams are clear, grounded, and focused on the priorities, behaviors, and outcomes that allow them to achieve their goals, then results and fulfillment in and outside of their work will quickly become their reality.

If you're ready and willing to do what it takes to achieve your goals and get what you deserve from your operation, then I invite you to turn the page and begin your journey. Keep in mind what motivational speaker Eric Thomas said, "Strategy is applauded and appreciated. Execution is worshipped." It's time to build upon your momentum and see your restaurant reach the next level.

CHAPTER 1

CRASH

"Adaptability is about the powerful difference
between adapting to cope and adapting to win."
—Max McKeown

I t's Wednesday, March 11, 2020.

I'm in a room with leaders from the Craft Beer Market. We're
hosting a three-day session in beautiful Vancouver, British
Columbia. It's been an incredible session so far, two days of
focused, powerful discussion pushing these amazing leaders to be
the best they can be. We're teaching them how to coach, we're putting strategy in place, and everyone's excited by how well it's going
and how charged up they feel.

But there's a buzz in the room. It's slight, but you notice
it. People are checking their phones more often during breaks.

They're leaving the room to take calls. And even though there's energy and excitement, faces are more drawn. Everyone looks just a little bit worried.

Turns out, COVID-19 is the subject of conversation. The word on the street is that the disease could shut our industry down. It is a gray cloud in that room for sure—but no one really believes it. Even as we talk to each other, there is this feeling of, "It couldn't possibly happen. They couldn't shut us down."

Thursday, March 12, is a half-day session, the wrap-up to our three-day training. This session is really meant to be the anchor for our time together. It gets people clear on what they've learned, what they need to do, and where they need to go. As we come in early in the morning, we see that someone's set up a board—one of those simple, blank whiteboards. And they're writing on it.

The company I was coaching for this three-day training is a highly event-driven business. They make a large percentage of their revenue through events. Someone had set up the whiteboard to record any events that got canceled that day. It was a joke, a bit of lightness to help with the COVID cloud we found in the room again that day. We went through our whole session with that whiteboard in the corner of the room. Every now and then, someone would go over and write on it.

Between 8:00 a.m. and 11:00 a.m., this company had $250,000 worth of corporate events canceled. In one day. And that's only the messages they could get from their event planners in their restaurants.

You know the rest of the story. March 13, the Canadian government shut the whole restaurant industry down. It happened *that* quickly. But it was the night of March 12 that I remember. I was sitting with the owners in Vancouver, British Columbia, and I could see this look in their eyes. This realization that this could *really* happen. They could close our industry. They could shut our restaurants. It had been unfathomable only hours ago.

I didn't plan to write a COVID-19 chapter in this book. When I began it, we thought we'd be moving through COVID and it wouldn't be needed. But based on its impact, duration, and longevity, there's value in addressing this pandemic. There are key learnings, COVID or not, that are applicable moving forward. If you don't want to wander back into this difficult space or if you feel like you're done with COVID-19 and you've dealt with it, skip the chapter.

If you're sticking around, then here's what we'll be looking at. We'll look at the reality we're facing now and what we learned. But most importantly, we'll be asking ourselves: What action can we take from here on? And how can we win on the other side?

THE HUMAN SIDE

At the beginning of the shutdown, there were a few numbers floating around. They were saying that 50 percent of restaurants would shut down due to COVID-19 or pandemic-related reasons. I was back home when I heard these numbers, and I'll be honest—they didn't bother me. I thought they were fear-based PR. I thought some of the restaurant associations were pushing these numbers out to create scarcity and create fear, in the hope that they could then create positive action.

But the truth is, they're real. These numbers have or will come true. In all likelihood, as you're reading this, 50 percent of restaurants in North America will have closed down due to the pandemic. That's tens of thousands of locations. Millions of staff affected. We're talking about communities losing their hearts— because these are the places where people go to create connection, where they meet with the ones they love or make memories. So many of these locations were the soul of a locality, their identity. By the time you read this, they'll be gone.

That's true whether we're talking of New York City or small-town Barrie, Ontario, Canada. Everywhere is looking at that same percentage of shutdown. Sixty-five percent of restaurants that are currently open—even with government subsidy—are experiencing loss. And 19 percent, again with government subsidy, are operating at breakeven.

The human cost of this really came home to me when I spoke with an old friend, Brye. Brye is the general manager at Flore & Pines, which is a beautiful local restaurant around the corner from me in Calgary, Alberta. When I say it's beautiful, I say it with the full judgment of having seen many restaurants around the world. I've known Brye for a while now; I actually did development and strategy work with her when she was working with another group. At the point I spoke with her, she was the new general manager of Flore & Pines and navigating the best she could through this pandemic.

I hadn't spoken to her for six or seven months. We saw each other when I visited the restaurant, and instantly I could see she was carrying a weight. I asked her how she was doing. Her father had just passed, she said, and she had not made it home in time to see him. I shared my own unresolved grief about my father's death. We were able to connect quickly over that.

Matt, she said, *for the third time during this pandemic, I've had to let all my people go.*

When you think of restaurants, it's easy to think of physical space. To imagine bricks and mortar and four walls. You hear 50 percent of restaurants are to shut down, and you see windows boarded, shutters pulled down, and signs changed. We don't tend to talk about the owner who's signed her house against the business loan. Or the manager who's stayed thirty-five years in this industry. Or the general manager now standing in front of me, watching her people go because she was forced to make that call.

That's the human cost of COVID-19. The incredible stress and impact of open, close, open, close. That unknown future. When I talk about statistics and impact in this chapter, I don't mean just the physical restaurants. I mean the people in our industry, this stress and weight on everyone involved. I mean how difficult it makes doing what we came here to do: serve the communities we work in by creating great hospitality experiences.

The weight Brye was carrying was heavy. *I had to do it right before Christmas*, she told me. *I know there's nothing I can do about it, but it's fucking hard. It hurts me. I'm worried that it hurts my people. And I'm worried it hurts their trust in me.*

I told her I had spoken to hundreds of people during COVID, and that 95 percent of them understand that something like this is not her fault. I wanted her to understand that she hadn't lost her people's trust; she had made the right decision for the team and for the business.

It was a quick conversation that went deep because we shared on a personal level, and that gave me the chance to give her permission to forgive herself. I told her a simple truth, and I am telling you now, because it's the one thing we needed to remember to get to the other side of this: we've been here before.

WE'VE BEEN HERE BEFORE

The restaurant industry has patterns—up and down, booming and challenging. It may not seem like it now, but there have been other times when our industry has gone through obstacles that seemed insurmountable. When we've had to let staff go, close down physical spaces, and reinvent ourselves. I want you to think about those times. Recall when we thought our industry was over, only for it to come back. Not only come back, but come back *thriving*.

We don't have to go back too far. Think about 2008. In 2008, the stock market crashed and we faced an unprecedented financial crisis across North America. At that time, my partners and I were operating our business out of Toronto. We had an office on Bay Street, which was the financial district of the city. When the crisis hit, we saw it destroy corporate offices on the street—we saw the impact literally play out in front of us. But our industry seemed insulated. Nothing seemed to have changed for us.

And then within ten business days, we saw sales plummet in 70 percent of our 200 restaurant accounts in the Toronto market. All of a sudden, the market was gone.

Absolute fear set in. People started to close their doors. Staff jumped to other industries. There was panic—of course there was panic. We'd never seen anything like this. And the truth is that the financial crisis *did* hurt. The restaurant industry *did* bleed. Restaurants that were profitable prior to the crisis had to close or eat into their cash flow that took years to accumulate.

But *after* the financial crisis, we saw a boom. The number of seats in every major city had reduced, so guests had less choice. That means that those restaurants that *did* manage to survive, the top performers, had more guests to fill their seats. The pie got smaller but the pieces got bigger for whoever made it out.

This isn't a one-off. We saw the same trend when "no smoking" hit our industry. There was real fear at the time that local pubs couldn't survive this. Your regular sports bar would never make it out alive. Why would people come to these places to watch a game or share a drink if they couldn't smoke? They'd just sit and smoke and drink in their garages; they'd gather together in their basements. They wouldn't need a pub.

But this wasn't a fact-based judgment. Yes, we did face a six-month blip as we transitioned into no smoking. And depending on where you are in North America, there may still be some impact of this on your community. But the industry rebounded. We still have pubs. We still have sports bars. And they're thriving.

If we want to be dramatic, we can go all the way back to Prohibition. Prohibition wiped out our industry. Nothing was left except diners and small breakfast joints. But it came raging back. The point of all these stories is to say: COVID-19 is difficult. Hugely difficult, with large-scale impact and real human cost. *But we have been here before.* We will come out of this stronger. We'll be stronger leaders, we'll have made stronger businesses, and we will have learned key lessons that will make this a healthier industry. I really do feel that within twelve to thirty-six months, our industry will be booming. And it will be an exciting industry for those that can fight through, for those who stay on the rollercoaster to come out the other side.

It matters that you remember this *now*. It's a subtle mindset shift, but I want you to step away from the feeling that the sky is falling or that this is doomsday. I want you to place COVID-19 in context—in that historical line of unprecedented disasters I just unpacked for you—and I want you to look forward to the other side of this. Only once you do will you see the potential in this pandemic. Only then will you be able to glimpse opportunity. And only then will you see what this pandemic has shown us about our industry and what it means to move forward—the key lessons we need to learn.

WHAT WE'VE LEARNED

Tony Robbins is a big influence in my life; ask anyone who knows me. I don't know the man personally, but I feel like I do. I've attended most of his workshops, but the two programs I made a substantial time investment in were his Business Mastery programs. The theme of the Business Mastery program that I attended in 2017 was *Winter Is Coming*. All businesses can thrive in the good times. All top-performing businesses can thrive in the average times. But the best businesses are prepared for winter.

For six days, twelve to eighteen hours a day, we talked about how winter is coming. How do we prepare our business so we can fight through the winter and evolve so that we can take *advantage* when the seasons turn again and spring and summer come back?

That was in 2017. Today, Robbins's seminar has never been more apt. Winter isn't just coming. It's here. I urge you to take Robbins's lessons to heart and look at this pandemic clearly. What has COVID-19 taught us about the state of our industry? What has it taught you about your business? What can you learn and how can you change?

Let me give you two examples. The first is one that anyone in this industry will be familiar with: mental health. Mental health in our field is poor. People are burned out and overworked. Many times, we're working opposite hours to our family and friends, so don't have the social support we need to rejuvenate. We're also in an industry surrounded by booze and, I hate to say it, drugs, for whoever chooses to take them. That means we're battling addiction and substance abuse. All that existed prior to COVID-19. And the conversations around mental health were gathering prominence before the shutdown. There was definitely a trend—especially on university campuses when we got a chance to coach their on-campus hospitality operations—to talk more and more about the mental health challenges of our profession.

But COVID-19 took those conversations to a whole new level. And that's not because the pandemic-related shutdown created our mental health problems. They existed prior to COVID-19. What it did do, though, is magnify them. It made the conversations more frequent. We've had brave people who have been louder in sharing their stories. And based on that, we're starting to take action. We're learning to stop and listen to our people, as leaders, to protect them from burnout. We're creating opportunities to safely support people so that if they do have mental health issues, they can come to us. As leadership teams, we're learning new structures—the right structures—for our people.

COVID-19 did that. It did it by bringing something that *already* existed to the forefront of the industry. It created visibility around the severity of our mental health challenges, and so it created the opportunity for us to change. These changes make us better; they prepare us to get through winter and also to thrive when spring arrives.

The second example takes us back to the statistic at the beginning of this chapter: 50 percent of restaurants in North America were projected to shut down due to this pandemic. That's terrible and heart-breaking. Great businesses were closing, which was a huge loss for this industry. But let's go back to the facts for a moment. Eighty percent of restaurants close in their first three to five years of operation. So there is a percentage of that 50 precent that would have shut down anyway, pandemic or no pandemic—they didn't have the topline revenue to make it sustainable. That's hard to hear, but it's true. We have thousands of restaurants in North America that signed a lease they're never going to be able to get out from under. We have thousands of locations that over-invested in their build-out. And worse, we have thousands of locations in the restaurant industry—tens of thousands—that have a handful of partners who don't have a proper partnership agreement and who wanted their money back before they opened their doors. And that's never going to happen.

I'm not taking away from the actual severity and crippling impact of COVID-19. But I believe at least *half* of that 50 percent of closures were going to happen anyway, just based on business fundamentals and the flawed structure of their business plan. That's not COVID-19's doing—those are problems that have existed long before this pandemic.

That's why I wrote this book. I didn't write it with COVID-19 in mind, but I did write it with the aim of making business better, stronger, and more resilient and to fix these structural problems in our industry. And all of the strategies in the book apply with or without COVID-19. They're your roadmap; they're what gets you out of this; they're what makes you better. All that COVID-19 has changed is that there's more urgency to take action. You now face more reasons for you to move in the direction of your goals to ensure your business not only survives but thrives on the other side of this.

HOW TO CHANGE YOUR MINDSET

Where do you begin? How do you get to thinking about this pandemic in a way that's useful for you and your business and allows you to grow from it?

The first thing I want you to do is put the reality of COVID-19 in a box. I understand that this is not easy—in fact, it's incredibly hard. My partners and I lived through this in our own business, asking ourselves, "Can we survive?" But as long as it's *out* of the box, all those negative impressions and real-life consequences will play on your mind. They'll affect the way you think and act, even what you see. Put it in a box so that we can control it. Once it's in the box, we can look at it honestly and see how our thought process is affecting our business and how we show up to our teams and ourselves. We can begin to see what's possible.

To do this, I have two simple exercises for you. The first thing I encourage you to do is think about three stories you've been telling yourselves about this pandemic. All of us have narratives we tell ourselves about the events in our lives. So what are the three things you are telling yourself about your business or the restaurant industry today?

For example, a lot of managers are saying to themselves, *I need to leave this industry because it's not stable. I can't trust it, and it's going to go away. So I need to leave as a manager—dump all my experience and shift over to becoming a mortgage broker or work in retail.* Another story I hear a lot from people is, *Guests are not going to come back into restaurants. They're not going to dine out again. We'll never get to see the numbers that we were seeing.* And some are even saying that restaurants are done. They'll never reopen, and the restaurant experience just isn't going to be part of the fabric of North America as it once was.

You don't have to have these stories, of course. Think about what you've been worrying about over the last year. You may be reading this well after COVID had passed into history, but I know there are still things that keep you up at night. What has the voice in your head been telling you? Write it down on a blank piece of paper. Take the time to put in any detail that seems relevant to you; capture those thoughts as clearly as you can.

Now, for each of these stories, I want you to write out the truth. What's the evidence that supports that this is actually happening? If you think all guests are going away, write down the fact that supports this story you're telling yourself. If you think there's no need for managers anymore, put down the statistics and evidence that tell you so.

What this exercise does is help you see clearly. As business owners or leaders, we're consistently creating stories about our business and our industry. Some are grounded, but some are just not true. Knowing which is which makes all the difference. Once you put some context and hard facts around those stories, you might be able to leave them behind. The fact is our industry *is* going to

WHAT ARE THE STORIES WE ARE TELLING OURSELVES?

STORY	EVIDENCE OR TRUTH TO SUPPORT THE STORY	✓ ✕
1.		
2.		
3.		
4.		
5.		

need great top-performing managers more than ever. My belief was that guests would return when we could convince them that we were safe. And once we had a vaccine, they were going to come running out of their homes and look for connection outside of the four walls that they'd been stuck in for the last year and a half. Restaurants are not done. They will always be part of our communities. They will always be a part of the fabric of North America and our connection as humans.

The second exercise I recommend will help you see that better. One of the large-scale impacts of COVID-19 is that we feel like *everything* has changed. But the truth is, while some things *have* changed, more has stayed the same. Take a blank piece of paper and write down five things that have changed inside your operation. It could be that you're now hiring via Zoom instead of through in-person interviews or you've had to reimagine service delivery. Write down *any* five things.

When you have this list of five things that have changed, take a fresh piece of paper. Now write down five things that have *not* changed for your business. What do you love doing that will stay the same? What are the five things you were doing that, when done consistently, led to greater success for your business?

I've done this simple exercise with many leaders, and the impact has been transformative. I went through it with a large university looking to bring back its students safely for 2021. The coaching session was with the multiple outlets across their campus—almost a dozen places ranging from quick service to pubs, restaurants, and cafes. All the conversation about reopening centered on plexiglass. *Where do we put the plexiglass up? We need to put stickers on the ground. We need to develop contract tracing apps.* There was this fear

COVID REFLECTION PLAN

WHAT HAS CHANGED BASED ON COVID?	WHAT HAS STAYED THE SAME AS YOU REOPEN YOUR OPERATION POST-PANDEMIC?
1.	1.
2.	2.
3.	3.
4.	4.
5.	5.
WHAT HAS THE IMPACT BEEN?	**HOW DO YOU RESET?**
1.	1.
2.	2.
3.	3.
4.	4.
5.	5.

in the conversation, and it hung like a black cloud over this great leadership team.

They were right, of course. They did need safety standards in place. They did need to update their training for their staff. But once they were done, I gathered them together. I did this exercise with them. I made them list what had changed—plexiglass was at the top of the list—and then I made them list what had stayed the same. And that's when it got exciting. They were able to shift away from the negativity of how COVID-19 had affected their operation and reground themselves in their catering and events training. They realized a lot would stay the same: Their company culture. How they engaged with their staff. Ninety percent of their service strategy and delivery.

And they got excited. This team had been winning so much before the pandemic—trending above the goals they'd set—and they thought COVID-19 had taken that away from them. But it hadn't. And once they realized that, their old positivity came over the group. They became electrified to move forward and tweak—not fundamentally change—who they were when they reopened their campus.

That possibility is yours as well. Question the stories you're telling yourself. Write down the hard facts of what will and won't change. Look to the other side of this so you may show up more meaningfully for your people and for your company, and start to reimagine change.

THREE LESSONS

I want to leave you with my three key takeaways from the COVID-19 shutdown. The nature of my job as a coach means I've immersed myself in the industry as we've moved through this pandemic; 80

percent of my week is talking to operators and leadership teams. I've watched leaders successfully navigate their way through the challenges, and here's what I've learned:

PIVOT, BUT WITHIN YOUR ORGANIZATION

"Pivot" has become a buzzword during this pandemic, but it's highly misunderstood. Most people think pivoting means you need to change yourself or your business model or find a new concept. But that isn't the case. What I encourage you to do if you're pivoting is to first pivot *within* your organization.

What do I mean by that? I mean: Don't change yourself. Just double down on what you're doing that already makes you great. So if you're doing guest service now, pivoting would mean: *We're not just going to have a guest service strategy. We're going to have the best guest service strategy designed for our guest avatar that will ensure we deliver remarkable experiences through third-party delivery or curbside pickup, all the way until we open our doors.*

This idea comes from a concept in Jim Collins's excellent business book, Good to Great. In it, he talks about the concept of "preserve the core and stimulate progress." To me, that phrase breaks down into two parts. When you preserve your core, you're making sure you're clear on what got you to this point of success. You're acknowledging it and ensuring you're fully committed to investing in what led you to this point. The second part, "stimulate progress," is about *adding* to your core. You don't move away from it; you complement it. You tweak what you're doing so that you're adding more value to what was already working.

That's what you need to focus on from here on out. Double down on what makes you great; don't pivot to something new.

NAVIGATE YOUR RELATIONSHIP WITH
THIRD-PARTY DELIVERY COMPANIES

Delivery has become a reality for everybody in the industry; there's no getting away from it. But you should be concerned about your large-scale delivery platforms: Uber Eats, DoorDash, SkipTheDishes. I have nothing against third-party delivery platforms. Love the companies, love the concept. We do coaching with two of those three brands. But I've also got into heated arguments on what their stance is.

Here's the concern with large third-party delivery platforms: if you're a restaurant operator, then the last thing you want is your guests going to a large platform in your small-town community and getting exposed to dozens of options instead of yours. It means they'll return to your business less, just based on the natural presentation of choice. And the number of options on that *one* platform is only going to increase as there's consolidation in the industry. There are not going to be more delivery providers in the coming years, but fewer.

If you're a restaurant operator reading this, then I want you to have a *passionate*, burning desire to ensure that you have a delivery strategy that lets you *own* your guests. If they order delivery, give them bounce-back coupons to bring them into your restaurant for their next visit. Provide an offer that leads them directly to you for curbside pickup. Give them the opportunity to be part of your restaurant group, loyalty programs, and your Facebook community. Stay connected with your guests so they don't become owned by third-party delivery companies. This is going to be one of the most damaging hangovers for many multisite operators, and we're going to start seeing its effects in twelve to thirty-six months as restaurants reopen. But there's opportunity to keep the power with you through simple strategy. At the end of the chapter, we've provided a link to a course that will show you how to own your customer.

WHO DO YOU NEED TO BECOME?

This last takeaway isn't an exercise, really; it's simpler than that: create thinking time for yourself as a leader or owner. Every day, I want you to set aside twenty to sixty minutes to think about who you need to become to make sure your business is set up for success. When restaurants reopened for indoor dining, what did your business need to be, not only to survive but to thrive? You'll need a few sets of this time investment to really get meaningful answers. I want you to think as granularly as possible. What does your hiring process look like? Your people development? How are you creating a great culture? How are you providing memorable experiences for your guests every time?

As you'll learn throughout this book, you don't need a long list of actions to arrive at meaningful answers. It's not about the next *twelve things you must do now*. Pare down. What are the one to three things you needed to do to be great once your restaurant reopened? That's all you need: one to three things. Spend the time thinking about it so that you're prepared for when the snow melts and spring is here.

WINTER IS YOUR SEASON

Everything I've said in this chapter is from the benefit of experience. I know the power of those two exercises I've talked about above because we did them in my own business when the shutdown first hit. We had two companies at the time: our coaching company and our profit-enhancing company. We had so many stories about what would happen to us. *The industry won't return. When it does return, it won't be able to afford our services.* We were telling ourselves stories about our sister company, Results Hospitality, and its focus on increasing profit for restaurants. We thought we would have to shut down based on questions about its viability—would the market need it post-COVID?

We finally re-anchored when we were able to look at what had changed and what had not. It led us back to these simple questions: What were we best at? What allowed our team to thrive? We rediscovered our core, which was incredible value-added customer service. And we doubled down on it. We decided to go all-in, no matter what happened. Even if the industry did implode and didn't open for another three years, we were going to do everything we could, not to sell to our clients, but to *add as much value* during the shutdown as possible.

Our belief was simple. If we didn't act aggressively with value-based solutions for our clients, or if we didn't have more to offer when the industry reopened, then we were at risk of going bankrupt. But if we did what we needed to drive value and stay connected to our clients, while reimagining who we needed to be when the industry reopened, we had a chance of thriving. So we leveraged our time during the shutdown to prepare. We innovated, created content, wrote books, and created online courses we didn't have before. And we did that because we got clear on the benefit. It wasn't about us, it was about the *value* we deliver to our clients. That anchored us through the journey and kept us close to our core.

The benefit was obvious. If we evolved, we had a thriving business for years to come. The risk if we didn't—if we didn't double down on our core and make those tweaks—was that we wouldn't exist in eighteen to thirty months.

The same benefit and risk face you now.

COVID-19 has been difficult for our industry, but it's also shown us what's been systematically wrong in the hospitality field. It's provided us a chance to change, to create new structures that won't crumble because they aren't riddled with the same old faults.

This book is your roadmap. It's time to create a business and culture that can survive through the winter—and it starts in our next chapter with making vulnerability your core.

✗

KEY TAKEAWAYS

- The duration, longevity, and impact of this pandemic on our industry have been vast. There are key learnings from this that are widely applicable moving forward.

- Fifty percent of restaurants were expected to shut down across North America due to COVID-19 or pandemic-related reasons. That's thousands of locations and millions of staff affected.

- But we've been here before. We've faced the financial crisis of 2008, handled the "no smoking" decree—and we even survived Prohibition.

- Many things in our industry were unhealthy prior to COVID-19. COVID-19 gives us a chance to talk about these aspects and effect real change.

- The key to tackling the pandemic is changing your mindset. Put COVID-19 in a box, and then evaluate the stories you're telling yourself about this pandemic and list what has really changed.

- There are three key lessons I want to leave you with:
  - Pivot, but within your organization.
  - Navigate your relationship with third-party delivery companies.
  - Ask, who do we need to become?

CHAPTER 2

VULNERABILITY-BASED LEADERSHIP

"Vulnerability is the birthplace of
innovation, creativity, and change."
—Brené Brown

H ere's what we're going to do, Jorge said. We're going to lead
with vulnerability.

I was working with the Woodbine Entertainment Group,
one of North America's largest horseracing and casino operations.
They operate multiple properties at large scale—huge, complex venues. At the time, we were working specifically with their hospitality
department. But we were running into challenges. We found that
the expectations we were creating for their hospitality leaders and

managers weren't being echoed in other areas of the operation. The only people acting out those expectations were the hospitality team members themselves.

And so they stopped. They didn't want to be vulnerable when no one else was going to follow their lead. They didn't want to put themselves out there like that, and I couldn't blame them.

Enter Jorge.

Jorge Soares was the senior hospitality leader at the time, and he's one of my favorite leaders that I've ever worked with, a passionate and connected person. Every time I met with him, I watched him say hi to five employees before he ever came and paid attention to me, his coach.

What Jorge decided to do to fix the problem was show his team how to lead with vulnerability. At the time, the departments at Woodbine Entertainment mainly functioned in silos. They kept their heads down, worked alone, didn't talk to each other, or even refer to each other in company meetings. That was the culture. Jorge showed how to create connection between departments with a simple, vulnerable step: they were going to say *hello* and acknowledge every *single* person from different departments as they continued to cross and communicate with them in the company.

Now, that may not sound like vulnerability to you. Most of us have intense definitions of vulnerability that involve some form of baring our souls. But that's the simplicity of vulnerability. Acknowledgment, hello, and asking people about themselves first— this has incredible power to create connection. Those simple gestures started a trend at Woodbine Entertainment that fundamentally changed the organization. They went from having enormous employee issues to making Canada's list of fifty best employers.

That's the power of vulnerability. It has the ability to transform organizations from the inside out by creating connection, trust, and communication that's the basis of innovation and growth. If you haven't seen Brené Brown's viral TED Talk, then I highly recommend you do. Brown's work has created a complete shift in how businesses run by showing us the requirement for vulnerability and conversations around shame and guilt. In her words: "Part of growth, innovation, and change is shame, vulnerability, and blame."

That's not easy for a lot of leaders to hear. Most people get uncomfortable just *reading* about vulnerability. Oftentimes, leaders have been taught *not* to be vulnerable, that we need to be proper role models who have all the answers and that we have to be perfect. Many even associate vulnerability with being weak or submissive (when they totally shouldn't). When Brown's TED Talk went viral, several Fortune 500 companies called her and said: *We love your talk, we love your content, we think you're funny. We love everything about you and we want to hire you—just don't talk about shame and vulnerability.*

And she laughed and said, *Shame and vulnerability are the foundation of change and growth.*

They are. If you want to scale your company, then you need to invest in vulnerability, and that has to start with the senior leadership. A lot of the companies I coach want their people to be more vulnerable, but they don't want to do it themselves. That isn't an option. If the leader is not willing to lead by example and display vulnerability consistently for a certain period of time, you can't expect your people to adopt that culture.

But if you *do* adopt vulnerability-based leadership, the results are incredible. When we can be vulnerable, we can have real connection with our people. When we have real connection with our people, we build trust. Trust allows us to get into positive conflict, which allows us to get to decision-making. By being vulnerable, we create the environment that allows us to make decisions, move forward with velocity and intention, and create the results that drive the team and the leader in the direction we need. It becomes the foundation of flow, joy, and purpose in the workplace.

Make no mistake—your people want you to be vulnerable. They *want* connection. They don't want "perfect" from their leaders; they want real and relatable. More than any title or organization chart, your people crave growth and connection. By being vulnerable and refocusing on connection in your organization, you can give them that.

In this chapter, we're going to discuss ways for you as a leader to get real—not only with yourself, but with your team.

It starts with building trust.

BUILDING TRUST

I love Patrick Lencioni; I've invested in almost every program he has. One of his most influential books, in my opinion, is *The Five Dysfunctions of a Team*. In it, Patrick talks about what an organization needs to function effectively and what, if missing, can cause it to fail. The five dysfunctions are essentially a pyramid broken up into five levels. The "absence of trust" is at the base of the pyramid, and it moves up through "fear of conflict," "lack of commitment," "avoidance of accountability," and finally to "inattention to results."

I want you to focus on that bottom tier of the pyramid: "absence of trust." If we don't start with a foundation of trust, we can't move forward in an organization. We *can't* create accountability. We *can't* create decision-makers. And ultimately, we can't create the results we all want and deserve. If you don't trust your people, you're not going to be able to let go to let them help you, and you'll be back to where you started at the beginning of this book: at capacity, overwhelmed, and unable to truly scale.

Lack of trust eats into every level of the organization. Without trust, employees are more likely to simply nod their heads and "yes" you to death. While that might avoid conflict, it certainly doesn't lead to excellence in execution or engagement. Lack of trust usually manifests itself by making everyone work harder without achieving any significant results. If you *have* a foundation of trust, however, then everyone is able to practice passionate positive conflict to move together in the direction of your goals.

So how do you create trust? Well, when Phil Jackson became the head coach of the Chicago Bulls, he couldn't just walk in and expect everyone to trust him. He first had to share his philosophies and experience and explain why he felt they were important for the success of the team. He had to *earn* Michael Jordan's trust because his methods were different than those of the previous coach. He did that by communicating openly and creating buy-in. He did it by being vulnerable.

When I was younger, I was very animated and emotional in my leadership style. My inconsistency didn't engender trust. In fact, it created a big disconnect between me and my team. I still remember walking into a meeting with Marcel, who was one of the core leaders at the time. We were going through a big innovation change and relaunch, and I was hoping to shock the team into taking action. I came into that meeting guns blazing. I brought all of my ideas to the table and all of my energy to push everyone into full throttle.

I thought I was helping. I really did. But Marcel stopped the meeting and asked, *Why are you yelling at me? What did I do wrong?*

I was so baffled by that. What the hell was he talking about? I was just trying to get this thing *moving*—why the fuck wasn't he in fifth gear already? I ended up pushing Marcel so hard that he quit the company. So did other people. And what I realized after I interviewed them is that they liked working with me, but they were never sure which Matt was going to show up. Would it be the Matt who was going to stop the meeting and give them a hug? Or the Matt who was going to be so excited about our vision, results, goals, and people that he'd break into tears? Or maybe it would be the Matt who was going to jump on the table because the company didn't hit a goal last week.

Consistency matters. In new relationships, trust is not a given; you have to earn it. If you want to create trust with your team, then you have to show up as a leader in a consistent manner. Let them know what to expect from you, and then deliver on those expectations. As I matured, I learned to do this. I now share *how* I operate with my team and with new hires so they always know where they stand. I tell them:

I operate from a position of uncertainty, as opposed to certainty. I have a goal to do in business what has never been done before. Ninety-five percent of people will not want to work with me or around me. But those that do will have an experience of a lifetime and will be taught how to grow and develop themselves as leaders. I can be extremely challenging to work for. We are going to do great things. But if you don't want to be on a roller-coaster or at a trajectory that's consistently up and striving for greatness, then I can tell you, we are not the team to join. I am not the leader you want to work with.

The impact is incredible. Simply sharing that gets people's buy-in. And we saved hundreds of thousands of dollars not hiring the most talented person in the room because the most talented person knew I was not someone they wanted to be around every day.

Don't wait for an incident like my meeting with Marcel to push you into changing. Find out what your people think of you now, and how you need to improve. A good exercise I recommend to my clients is in *Think and Grow Rich* by Napoleon Hill. It's called "See Yourself as Others See You." Give it to five people you truly care about and who know you, and have them write a reflection of how you show up. Trust me, it's transformative. (I first did it when I was in my twenties and found it deeply helpful.) It gives you a foundation to get grounded and understand where you need to change. The ability to see yourself as others see you is a critical foundation of growth, trust, and engagement with your team.

Also work on creating a space in your company for people to be honest and to develop trust. Spend more time listening to your team and creating connections. This open communication is key to the success of your business. You'll be surprised by the number of companies that don't do this. I once held a coaching session with the Distillery District Restaurant Corporation. After the session, Rik, the vice president of the Distillery Restaurant Group, called me up and asked me how it went. I told him it went great.

Good, he said. *I've had a chance to connect with all my people, and I've got a problem I want to talk to you about.*

I wasn't sure what the problem would be, but I was open to listening.

Matt, he said. *I didn't hire you to make my people cry. I need you to stop doing it if we're going to work together.*

What I had done in that session was create a space for trust and for people to be vulnerable with each other. What sparked that deep emotion from a few people is that I asked them how they were doing.

That's it.

No one at work had stopped to ask them that question. When I asked and showed that I cared, they reacted deeply and with emotion.

I told Rik, *That emotion was there in your business before I asked the question. By asking, we were able to take the pressure off and create some space that allowed us to move forward with trust and vulnerability.*

Once I was able to clarify what was happening, Rik understood. There was full buy-in from him that we need to check in with our people to see how they're doing. I encourage you to create space for these open conversations and to allow your people to be seen. During COVID-19, we needed these spaces more than ever.

I'll leave you with one last thought about trust. Growth and development always start with you. Be vulnerable and tell your people you're working on your leadership skills and that your approach may change as a result—you might start asking different questions and engaging differently. Explain that the reasoning behind this shift is to strengthen the organization, culture, and business results. Your employees will appreciate your efforts and respond in kind.

PUBLISH YOUR INTENTIONS

As you read this book, you're going to evolve and grow as a leader. You're going to have ideas about the changes you want to make, the new patterns of behaviors you want to adopt, and the different paths your organization is going to follow.

The one thing I encourage you to do is publish those intentions with your team. This means any macro changes, such as new directions, philosophies, and ways of working, and it also means micro changes, such as the transitioning of a role or adjustments in your behavior. If you change your role and your junior manager who is used to seeing you once a day no longer sees you, that's going to confuse them. And it could scare them, even if the change is positive and good for the company. So take the time to explain what you're doing and why so that your team understands.

There are several other benefits to publishing your intentions. It makes you accountable to your team, and lets them hold you up to the new standard. Most importantly, it signals your ongoing commitment to these changes. You can't expect your staff to believe your new behaviors the moment you start doing them. Signaling your commitment is therefore important. Respect the process: you're going to have to show up that way consistently for two or three months before they really buy into the leader you've become.

I know this because I've seen it happen. I was working with a thirty-plus location group that was nationally operated and had a large footprint. As I built trust and a relationship with the leader, I found that the person was working through substance abuse issues. And because he was trying to hide his overload and his stress, he started to isolate himself from his team.

This leader's team *loved* him. They knew he had substance abuse issues, they saw him isolate himself from them, and they wanted to help. They wanted to reach out and create engagement. But no one had ever talked about the problem openly, and so they weren't able to open dialogue about it. It was just *there*, this elephant in the room no one could address.

To solve this, we created a space to break open the topic. We didn't go into details of the substance abuse challenge—that level of sharing wasn't needed. But what we did was create a space for the leader to share with his team that he knew he wasn't showing up as consistently as he knew he could or should. By being vulnerable and sharing where he was at and how he was committing to move forward, that leader lit a *fire* under his team. By the end of that sixty-minute meeting, his team would have run through a wall for him. He did it by being vulnerable about a situation that everyone was aware of but nobody was talking about.

SHUT UP AND LISTEN

Connection doesn't happen by telling people what to do. If you're an owner who used to be in charge of hiring staff, for example, and your first reaction when a manager tells you they are having trouble finding good employees is to share how you used to do it, you're doing it wrong. Don't imprint your beliefs on your employees. Instead, aim to empower them to come up with their own creative solutions.

For many leaders, this can be quite the challenge. In our quest to fix problems and move our businesses forward, we jump to solve each problem with what we think is best, using our own vast experiences and insight. Resist this urge. Give your managers and your employees the opportunity to come up with solutions to problems on their own.

One of my clients, Dave, used to run three large restaurants with over $25 million a year in revenue. He's a fast-moving leader, someone who thinks quickly on his feet—one of the smartest people I know. Dave had created a culture where his people could do *nothing* without him. They'd ask him about the smallest things. *What should we do about the menu? Or the new patio design? How do we fix that job ad? What type of napkins should we buy?*

Rather than position his people to make a decision based on his experience, Dave answered those questions for every single person. And so his people thought he wanted to make every decision by himself. It created a paralyzing experience for Dave. When he went into the venues, he was immediately bombarded with a lineup of people with questions. It upset his team. They felt undervalued. They felt micromanaged. They felt disengaged.

What Dave's people needed from him wasn't an answer to their questions. They needed his empathy. His *time*. Vulnerability is listening to someone's question and *relating* to it. It's listening to their challenge and perhaps sharing an experience where you grappled with a similar problem. It's acknowledging that there is an issue—the menu does need to be fixed—and empowering them to find their own way forward. If you're not willing to get to somebody's level and if you're just willing to spit out an answer, I promise it will create *dis*connection, not connection.

That's what happened with Dave. As a result, he battled with 200 percent annual staff turnover and short staff in some of the busiest restaurants in North America. It was an unsustainable business model driven by a lack of vulnerability.

To truly engage, create buy-in, build trust with your people, take a step back, and slow down. Listen fully to the issue. Empathize. Tell your manager you understand how stressful it can be finding quality hires, and how you went through similar experiences at that stage of your career. Only then is it time to talk solutions— and those should be made collaboratively and enable you both to move through the situation together.

When you welcome your managers and your staff to take part in solving problems, they not only feel heard and respected, but you're also giving them a sense of ownership in your operation. This shifts their perspective on their role within the company, often in a more positive and engaging direction. When you approve their proposed solutions, you're sending them the message that you trust them, planting the seed that you value them and their contributions.

This will only make them want to be more involved in your operation.

FORGET PERFECTION

Perfection is not attainable. Most leaders want to be perfect, and they push their businesses to be the same, but perfection isn't possible. Think about this for a second. Microsoft launches beta versions of their programs and operating systems to hundreds of millions of people around the world that are incomplete. These are some of the most-used applications in the world, and Microsoft rolls out incomplete versions of them so that they can get feedback from the consumer to make it right. If we push for perfection, we can get lost in it. Perfection is *slow*, and perfection creates disconnection from results and decision-making.

Most leaders think they have to always present perfection to their employees. They are completely different behind closed doors than they are in front of their people, just like the owners I encountered while working for Labatt Breweries, now owned by Anheuser-Busch breweries. All smiles and false bravado on the outside, struggling on the inside.

This was my biggest challenge as a new coach. As I launched my business and became an entrepreneur, *I* was the leader who thought my people wanted me to have the answers, perfectly, every time. I thought they wanted me to be involved in *every* decision. As I write this, I can see how ridiculous it sounds, but at the time, I really believed it. I was young, I was hard-charging, and we were experiencing great success in the company. But my inability to listen, connect, and focus on people was costing our business.

At the time, one of my dearest friends in life worked for us: Nick Lecuyer. Nick joined us from Coca-Cola to do sales. Due to my immaturity, inexperience, and *conviction* that I always had to be right, I constantly drowned out his feedback. I ignored how we could improve the company.

Nick left. He moved on to start one of Canada's most successful independent mortgage brokerages. I lost my best friend because I wanted to be right. Because I thought I *had* to be. And the impact on my company was huge. We lost months—if not years—of growth and momentum through collaboration because I couldn't let go of being perfect.

When I finally decided to be a vulnerability-based leader, everything changed. The old me thought that when I had that nice suit on and wore those shiny shoes, I had to transform into someone who could fix anything. I wasn't genuine. I wasn't authentic. I wasn't listening—which Nick made very clear. It created *disconnection* from the people I was working with. When I chose to be vulnerable, I shared my story of how I grew up with divorced parents and alcohol abuse in my family. I talked about my learning disabilities and how my parents went to jail. I showed up as my true self.

It created significantly stronger connection with my team. I found myself working with people who wanted to make true change, and I learned how I could support them. (That was my role: I was there to support them; I wasn't there to *be* the change.) During that year-plus I was coached to be my true self, my company doubled in size.

If this same kind of belief system about perfection is holding you back, consider shifting your mindset. Allow yourself to be seen by the people who work for you. Vulnerability is the simple things: it's taking the time to connect and ask questions beyond the basic job to make sure there's human-to-human connection. It's being present. It's listening. It's letting go of perfection. That's it.

Enhancing your emotional range in professional situations is a process. Ease into it, tell your true stories, and allow people to connect with you. Your reward will be increased employee engagement and enhanced company culture.

THREE WAYS TO BE A MORE VULNERABLE LEADER

1. Create the space to have conversations with people to check in honestly.

2. Share your challenges. This is especially crucial now that we're on the other side of a pandemic. A lot of leaders will tell their people what they did to get stronger during COVID-19, and I encourage you to do that. But I also want you to share the challenges you faced. Showing up to your people to say, *There is no kink or challenge; keep fighting*—that doesn't empower them. The best way to support your team through this is to share an example of your challenge.

3. Take ownership of your faults. If your company is working on a major goal or project and you don't achieve it, one of the ways to be vulnerable is to share what you could have done better to help your team get a better result. Own what you could have done differently as a leader, and share what you will commit to doing differently in the future. It will create space for people to hear your vulnerability as well as share theirs.

WE ARE ALL HUMAN

While it's true that restaurants are in the service business, the most important thing we offer is human connection. We must remember that we exist in a human-to-human industry: the only way we deliver results is through consistent human-to-human behavior in the direction of our goals. If we forget this and stay solely focused on delivering results, we're setting ourselves up for failure.

Focusing on the human refocuses our attention on people and connection. As Brené Brown says, vulnerability and authenticity are at the root of human connection—and human connection is often dramatically missing from workplaces.

Create that connection. As a coach, I've found the biggest thing employees want is for their senior leaders to *slow down*. They want us to sit down for a coffee or a beer and have a conversation with them. Remember Jorge Soares from Woodbine Entertainment? Jorge understood this. He knew how critical human-to-human connection was for everybody on the team. He was the senior leader of operations who would stop and talk to the union busboy who had been there eight years. He would know his name. The buy-in that was created from his people was incredible. People want us to do our jobs, but they also want us to slow down and connect.

Here's a prime example. One of the leaders I was working with was leaving his office on a Friday—grabbing his bag, running down the stairs. And two of his employees blocked the stairs. They were holding up a six-pack of beer. They said, *Things have been so nuts over the past six months. Do you have time to stop and have a beer?*

The leader was running somewhere—but he was *always* running somewhere. So he stopped and had that beer. He could see the importance in it. Since then, we've scheduled time consistently in his company to catch up with the team. It's not about the beer—it's about the time.

Always remember that everyone is going through something. Me, you, the line cooks, the dishwashers, the servers, and the managers. In my continuous efforts to be vulnerable, I often share my struggles in presentations. It creates a space for people to open up about what's burdening them. For example, in my team, I shared that my wife and I had a miscarriage. I shared this because I knew my emotion was off—it was affecting me and my wife, and it was therefore affecting what I could bring to work. I found out that on my very small team, three of my people had had miscarriages inside of the last eighteen months. It wasn't about cracking into our personal lives—I didn't ask anybody to share if they had one. But by me simply sharing that, we deepened our connection and were better able to understand and support each other.

Taking the time to recognize that we're all human showing up in the four walls of a restaurant helps build stronger relationships all around. You don't have to be best friends with your employees, but making them feel seen and heard leads to mutual understanding and respect. Once that connection is there, everyone can have each other's backs and do whatever is needed to make the business successful. Remember, you don't have to force people to share. That's not the point of this. We're not asking people to talk about substance abuse and the extremely challenging experience of having a miscarriage if there's no trust in the group. If someone doesn't want to go deep, that's absolutely okay. Your role as a leader is to set expectations, and then let your people share what they want.

If we structure these conversations properly, people *will* share. The key is to implement a process that makes your team feel safe and believe there is a genuine space for them. Here are three processes we use that might help you as well:

PATRICK LENCIONI'S THREE QUESTIONS EXERCISE

One of the best exercises to start the process of having a vulnerable conversation with your team is the Three Question Exercise from Patrick Lencioni's *The Five Dysfunctions of a Team*. All you do here is have people ask each other three simple questions:

1. Where did you grow up?
2. Do you have any siblings, and where do you fall in that order?
3. What is an interesting or unique experience from your childhood?

We ran this exercise with a national restaurant group. Their leaders were in their mid-thirties to mid-forties, and they'd all been with the organization between fifteen and twenty years. When we added it up, it turns out they had a total of 450 years of experience with the company.

We broke the room up into groups of eight, and each group discussed the three questions among themselves. At the end of the exercise, this team—thirty people with a collective experience of 450 years with the company—said that they learned things about their co-workers and their best friends that they never knew.

Vulnerability starts with simple conversations. Just knowing where people come from and how they got here has huge potential to generate connection.

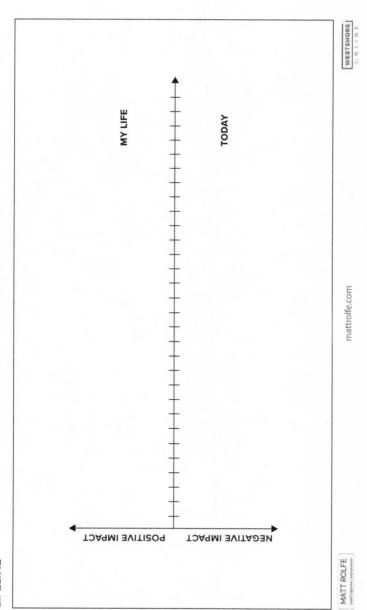

LIFELINE

MY LIFE

TODAY

NEGATIVE IMPACT POSITIVE IMPACT

WESTSHORE
ONLINE

mattrolfe.com

MATT ROLFE
COACH | SPEAKER | ENTREPRENEUR

LIFELINE EXAMPLE

Good times

Ok

Distress

Age

0 — 10 — 20 — 30 — 40 — 50

Birth of sibling
Start school
Join school team
Change school
Pass final exams
Leave school
Start college
Leave college
Get married
Start new job
House move
First child
Parent ill
Promotion
Second child
Redundant
Change career
Death of parent
Child starts university

mattrolfe.com

THE LIFELINE EXERCISE

This exercise is a bit deeper.

On a piece of paper, draw a timeline that starts at where you were born and ends at today. On that timeline, mark the important experiences in your life. I have done this exercise personally in Entrepreneurs' Organization as well as with dozens of groups and teams. It is *the* most powerful team connection exercise you can do—when the team is ready for it.

What it allows the team to do is trace *common* experiences across their lives. You start to see patterns emerge. Every guy, for example, usually had a low point between high school and college when a girl left them and broke their heart. That common link creates *connection*. Again, people only need to share what they're comfortable with. But just the act of writing those experiences down and realizing those connections is such a powerful way for us to understand each other. From a human-to-human perspective, it creates incredible bonding as a team.

THE HUMAN NEEDS EXERCISE

I learned this exercise from Tony Robbins when I attended his Business Mastery programs. According to Robbins, there are six fundamental human needs that people operate from: certainty, variety, significance, connection, growth, and contribution. In this exercise, we ask people to share the *two* human needs they connect with most right now. What do they feel most represents them in the workplace? Then we get them to share what their two *personal* driving needs are and how that might show up at work.

This exercise is critical for us to understand why somebody is acting in a certain way. Someone in your team may get really frustrated

HUMAN NEEDS EXERCISE

SIX HUMAN NEEDS	WHAT TWO HUMAN NEEDS CONNECT WITH YOU THE MOST?	WHY?
1. Certainty The need to know that you can avoid pain and gain pleasure	1.	
2. Uncertainty The need for the unknown, change, new stimuli		
3. Significance Feeling unique, important, special, or needed		
4. Love/Connection A strong feeling of closeness or union with someone or something	2.	
5. Growth An expansion of capacity, capability, or understanding		
6. Contribution A sense of service and focus on helping, giving, and supporting others		

if a payroll process isn't followed. We may think they're just nit-picking, but the reality is that they operate in certainty. Understanding where they're coming from will help us relate and connect more.

I once had the opportunity to work with one of my favorite development leaders, Katherine Oliver, on a huge project. But our challenge was that I operate fundamentally in uncertainty—as you know from my speech to my team—and Katherine operates in certainty.

Three weeks into our program, I was on a Zoom call with her and I could see an arm in the side of the frame. There was another person there, who turned out to be the VP of HR. Katherine was so frustrated with me because she couldn't understand where I was coming from that she'd brought her VP of HR onto the call to try to end the program.

We did this exercise together, and we explained both of our motivators. And by simply understanding each other, we were able to move forward to implement one of the most impactful programs I've ever coached with a client.

MAKE VULNERABILITY INTENTIONAL

You may be surprised to learn that the persona portrayed on television by multiple-Michelin-starred chef Gordon Ramsay is not who he really is. In real life, he doesn't yell at his employees or rage on in his business dealings. He's actually built a remarkable brand by being a kind-hearted and inspirational leader.

Jon Taffer is another example. The explosive personality you see on *Bar Rescue* is purely for entertainment. His incredible success as a restaurant consultant is based on the way he helps clients build culture through positive leadership.

The days of being hard-handed with staff and chefs are over. Leaders who use intimidation as their main tactic only alienate their workforce. If you want to build a company that will last, you need to focus on creating connection with your people—and that begins by placing vulnerability at your core.

Vulnerability-based leadership is the only way to engage and grow trust in your team. When you have trust, you have connection and positive conflict, and that creates an environment that pushes decisions and allows you to drive results toward your goals. But it has to begin with you, the leader. Show up as your authentic self. Create a space for your team to share and connect. And if you do, your organization will have a strong heart in place.

Once you've developed your core with vulnerability-based leadership, it's time to think about how to scale your company to the heights you want. Growth only happens with crystal clear vision—so let's see how you can develop one.

✕

KEY TAKEAWAYS

- Vulnerability is at the core of growth and innovation for businesses.

- We exist in a human-to-human industry: the only way we deliver results is through consistent human-to-human behavior in the direction of our goals.

- Vulnerability has to be present in the senior leadership of a company. If you're unwilling to lead by example, your people won't adopt this culture.

- A foundation of vulnerability creates flow, joy, and purpose in an organization.

- A foundation of trust is key to fostering vulnerability and creating an organization that can progress toward its goals.

- Leaders must show up consistently in order to earn their team's trust. Be upfront with your people on what they can expect from you.

- Connection doesn't happen by telling people what to do. Connection happens by listening, empathizing, and understanding where your people are coming from.

- Perfection is slow, and perfection creates disconnection from results and decision-making.

- People don't want their leaders to be perfect. They want them to be real and relatable; they want your true self.

- Slow down to have a beer or coffee with your team. They value your time.

· Three exercises that can help you shape a vulnerable
  conversation among your team are:
  → Patrick Lencioni's Three Questions Exercise
  → The Lifeline Exercise
  → The Human Needs Exercise

CHAPTER 3

ON VISION: CLARITY IS POWER

"Greatness starts with a clear
vision of the future."

—Simon Sinek

From 2005 to 2010, the Eastern Coast of Canada saw a lot of incredible chains from the West Coast expand into their territory. These West Coast chains had great concepts. They had beautiful designs and engaging staff. Overall, they gave off a sleek and sexy feel—an impression of stepping into a new, polished age.

The East Coast restaurants hit the panic button.

Now, these East Coast restaurants were already great. They were successful chains loved by many. But they looked at themselves, then looked at the West Coast restaurants, and panicked. They decided the only way to compete was to become their competition. They began mirroring exactly what the West Coast restaurants were doing.

Lights. Décor. Uniforms. Service. All the same.

There came a point where I could wander into *any* of the eight major multisite restaurants from the East Coast and not be able to tell the difference. They were identical. They all had different concepts—or at least they claimed to—but I couldn't tell you if it was a Moxie's, a Cactus Club, an Earls, or a Turtle Jack's.

They'd lost their vision.

At the time, we were working with Turtle Jack's Muskoka Grill. Muskoka is a place in Canada that almost everyone knows: beautiful scenery, with a real pristine atmosphere. Muskoka Grill had a "cabin feel" that worked with its surroundings. When the West Coast restaurants expanded into the East Coast, Turtle Jack's Muskoka Grill moved away from that feel. It became chic and sexy. All the staff wore black uniforms. Most of their staff became female, instead of a mix between male and female. They lost their identity.

I want you to think about the cost of that for a moment. When you're redeveloping a restaurant to look modern, you're looking at new TVs, new lights, and state of the art décor. That's a one to two million dollar extra investment per location. Now multiply that by twenty or fifty locations for a large-footprint restaurant chain. That's a lot of money spent rebranding to fit a concept that's not you—it's money poorly invested in the direction of *someone else's* goal.

And it's not money you make back easily. Your rebranding has taken you away from your identity, so now you've lost your competitive edge in the market. You're just like everyone else. Turtle Jack's Muskoka Grill saw sales declining north of 10 percent once they were competing with Earls or JOEY and their concept felt the same.

That's the cost of losing sight of your vision. When you don't have *clarity* about who you are and where you're going, your business suffers. It's not enough to simply have beautiful buildings or a good service experience anymore. To be successful in the hospitality industry, you have to 100 percent know where your business is heading and why. Although Turtle Jack's Muskoka Grill got off track, once they lasered back into delivering what they called "cottage hospitality," sales recovered.

In this chapter, I'm going to help you find that clarity, which starts with finding your why.

FINDING YOUR WHY

When I was twenty-five years old, I defined success pretty clearly. To me, it was measured by: How many hours could I work? How *hard* could I work? And could I sustain this high-frequency, maxed-out level of energy every single day that I showed up?

Then my financial partners gifted me a copy of Napoleon Hill's *Think and Grow Rich*, and everything changed. The book showed me that what I thought was my definition of success was actually someone else's. I was climbing somebody else's ladder. You know those gold stars they hand out for doing a good job? That's what I kept reaching for. And I wasn't going to find satisfaction that way because I wasn't clear on where I was and where I needed to go.

The impact of learning this at the critical age of twenty-five was immense. Using *Think and Grow Rich*, I was able to redefine what I really wanted for my future. Was I willing to achieve my results at work and end up with an empty personal life? Was I willing to lose my girlfriend at the time because I was pouring everything I had into the job? The answers to both questions were no. The book helped me see that and shape a new path. Because I could define who I wanted to become, I was able to create a clear and focused approach to get there. And based on *that*, I was able to refocus where I invested my time and energy to make sure I achieved those results.

In his Business Mastery series, Tony Robbins talks about the "reticular activating system" (RAS). What this means, essentially, is that our brains are programmed to block out most of what they see. If we were able to absorb everything we see and hear, our brains would explode. So our brains limit what we notice.

Our aim should be to program our RAS to focus on *what matters most*. Think of it like a cruise missile with a target. If you set your target correctly and launch your cruise missile, it's going to hit the bullseye. It doesn't matter if it faces an obstacle; it'll just change direction to avoid it before getting right back on track. What matters is *knowing* that target.

As Tony Robbins says: *Clarity is power.*

It's the same for restaurants. Most business owners launch their business—regardless of the industry—after identifying what they believe is a gap in the market. The reality for restaurant entrepreneurs, however, is that there's not a city, town, state, or province in North America that *needs* another restaurant.

So why do you exist?

Getting clear on that *why* is paramount. If you don't have one, find it. If you do, revisit it. Most top-performing multisite restaurant operators and owners created their "why" statements when they began their business. They haven't referred to it since. That's what happened to Turtle Jack's Muskoka Grill. When they faced competition from those West Coast restaurants, they didn't go back to their why to see how they could overcome these obstacles—exactly like a cruise missile—and still stay true to themselves. Instead, they moved away from their "why." And as we saw, it led to disaster—an overall decline in sales north of 10 percent. When we started working with them to fix this, the first thing we did is move them back to cottage hospitality. We got rid of the sleek interiors and the black uniforms. The restaurant went back to that cottage feel true to the venue. And in time, they were able to define a version of hospitality and service that aligned with their identity.

The results? Now that they've come back to who they are, they're outperforming those West Coast restaurants.

So even if you have created your why statement, revisit it. Take a step back and get crystal clear on the goals and vision for your business. To begin, determine the Purpose-Driven Questions on the following page for your restaurant.

Identify why each matters. All your answers will help you clarify exactly the type of guests you are looking for as well as the niche you are targeting. Staying grounded, true, and genuine in finding your why allows you to stand out in the market.

For example, it could be that your guests want value-based food quickly, to entertain their kids, and to use their mealtime as a way to connect with their significant other. To support that experience, you'd want to teach your servers to kneel down and get on eye level

PURPOSE-DRIVEN QUESTIONS

1. WHY DOES YOUR RESTAURANT EXIST?

2. WHO DO YOU SERVE? WHO ARE YOUR CORE GUESTS?

3. WHAT UNDERSERVED NICHE IN THE MARKET ARE YOU LOOKING TO FILL?

with little ones to help place the order, give out crayons, and have a toy chest available.

This kind of targeted service happens by design, not as a fluke. Clarity of vision and intention ensures your execution is in direct alignment with your strategy.

Let me give you an example. We were working with Pizza Nova, which is a family-owned and -operated quick service operation with over 150 franchised locations. We helped them get clear on their intention and execution by redefining their service strategy. And by that, I mean we first got clear on what experience they wanted to create for every single guest that interacted with them— either in store or through a delivery experience. We wanted to understand: where does Pizza Nova fit into the market? Where does it rank with its competition?

What we found was that Pizza Nova was already leading on product quality. But in order to charge the price points their product warranted, they needed a service experience that distinguished them from the rest. One of Pizza Nova's largest competitors is Dominos, and Dominos has a very large marketing budget. To compete, Pizza Nova had to stand out. The one way to do that was to create a unique service experience their franchisee network could implement consistently.

We designed a three-step service strategy known as "Welcome, Wow, Ciao." Roughly, it translated into:

- *Welcome* was about how Pizza Nova greeted their guests in store, at home, and online and made them feel at home.
- *Wow* focused on creating a unique experience the guest wouldn't forget. It answered the question: how did we wow them?

- And *Ciao* was based on the Italian concept and focused on how Pizza Nova ended the experience with the guest. We wanted to make sure they didn't just deliver and let the guest walk away but instead created a return guest and perhaps even a loyal one.

Welcome, Wow, Ciao. Simple but powerful. Their franchisees could get behind the strategy—indeed, they were *excited* by it because they could see how it made them different. But most importantly, the service experience, when delivered either through a call center or at the door, marked a completely different interaction with Pizza Nova for guests. And that had a direct effect on Pizza Nova's business; they continued to see double-digit growth in one of the most competitive sectors in the hospitality industry.

GOAL SETTING DISCIPLINE

Once you've clarified your vision, ideal guest, and reason for existing, the next thing to focus on is creating simple, clear, execution-focused one- and three-year plans for your restaurant. Moving forward with intention is critical. Remember the spin cycle we talked about in the Introduction? It's essential you don't keep spinning between Awareness and Choice; you must move down to Decision to get results. These plans help you do that. They take some time to craft, but they're worth it. Most people spend more time planning their vacation than their goals—don't be one of them!

One thing to keep in mind as you go through the one-year plan and three-year plan is the Rule of Three. So many of us believe that in order to achieve success or get to that next level, we need to have ten, twelve, or fifteen goals for the year. We think that's the only way we're *really* moving forward; that's real progress.

But it's just not true. Research has shown—and there are proven statistics—that if teams have more than three focus goals, they move from being able to complete things at an excellent level to not really being able to meet expectations. Their focus is too diversified. The Rule of Three for me is essentially: *let's not overcommit.* What are three critical focuses, projects, and service steps that if you did *consistently* and *relentlessly* would allow you to achieve your goals? Three is all you need and is the optimal number.

You'll see the Rule of Three crop up again and again in the plans below. Honor it. Trust me, it'll make a remarkable difference in your personal, team, and company results.

YOUR ONE-YEAR PLAN

The idea behind your one-year plan is that you should be able to set down your strategy for the year clearly, simply, and on a single page. The following page shows what a one-year-plan looks like.

As you can see, it consists of a double spread. Let me talk you through the overall layout before we dive into each element. On the left-hand side, you have the tactical and results-driven aspects of your one-year strategy: (1) your "how to win" statement, also known as "rally cry" or "core focus"; (2) your critical drivers; and (3) your core projects. On your right-hand side, you list elements that will help your team buy into your tactical and results-driven goals and that reflect the human side of your organization—in other words, the emotional elements everyone can get behind. That's (1) your core values and (2) your commitments.

ONE PAGE STRATEGTIC PLAN | 1-3 YEARS

WHY STATEMENT

HOW WE WIN/RALLY CRY/CORE FOCUS: 12 MONTHS

CRITICAL DRIVERS: RULE OF THREE

What	Who	When
1.		
2.		
3.		

CORE PROJECTS: WHAT/WHY/WHO/WHEN

What	Why	Who	When
1.			
2.			
3.			
4.			
5.			

STRATEGY EXECUTION QUESTIONS

Why does your restaurant group exist?

Who do you serve? Who is your core guest?

What underserved niche in the market do you serve?

THREE CORE GUESTS

1.
2.
3.

HOW DO WE GET THERE?

1. _____ 2. _____ 3. _____
1.
2.
3.

YOUR COMMITMENTS

What's your commitment to your employees?

What's your commitment to your guests?

What's your commitment to you community?

What's your commitment to your self?

mattrolfe.com

MATT ROLFE

WESTSHORE
O N L I N E

Let's tackle these in more detail.

The first thing I want you to be able to define for your business is: how do you win? You need to describe what success looks like. What's the result you're looking to achieve that lets you celebrate at the end of the year? That celebration could be a ski trip with your team or popping open bottles of Champagne—that's up to you. What matters is that everyone is crystal clear on what that result looks like.

The reason Michael Jordan and Tom Brady have been so successful is that they always knew exactly what they were trying to achieve. They knew they wanted to be holding the championship trophy at the end of the season. They knew exactly what success looks like.

That's the difference between aiming for the playoffs and aiming for the trophy.

We call this description our "how to win" statement. It's also known as our "rally cry" and our "core focus," just to give operators three options to choose from to make sure the language lands with their teams. It's one to two sentences, at maximum, that provides a clear example of what success looks like, along with some indication of how it may be measured.

One of our clients had the rallying cry of "ten up while we tighten up," meaning they were aiming for 10 percent sales growth while they tightened up their processes. The year LeBron took the Cleveland Cavaliers to victory in the NBA finals, their rally cry was "all in." Another one of our clients used the core focus of "get it done." They found that a lot of their core projects were being held up at the 80 percent mark and so their rally cry translated into, *let's get it done, let's get it executed, and let's see results.*

VISION STATEMENT VS.
YOUR WHY STATEMENT

There's a subtle difference between your vision statement and your why statement. Your vision statement deals with where you are going. It's the exact destination or result you've probably noted in your one-year plan or your three-year plan (which we tackle in the next section). Your why statement, however, deals with a simple question: why does achieving that result matter?

Say you put down your vision statement as: *we want 12 percent net profit next year.* Sounds great; that's a big number. Your why statement deals with: why should anybody give a shit about achieving that goal? The answer could be something along the lines of: *12 percent net profit will allow us to reinvest in stores and our people, which will allow us to open more stores.* That gets your leaders' and people's buy-in.

Vision is the clarity of where you want to get to. Your why statement is connecting with why anyone should care about it.

VISION AND WHY EXERCISE

VISION STATMENT

In a defined timeline, typically one to three years, what are the clear goals that you want to achieve?

Size of the organization
1. Number of employees
2. Number of customers
3. Number of countries

Products or services you offer the market

Position in the industry

Revenue/profit/growth potential

WHY STATEMENT

Why should your employees/customers buy into the goals?

Growth and development

Influence

Drive and commitment to be the best you can be

Fuel and support your growth

mattrolfe.com

MATT ROLFE

WESTSHORE
ONLINE

The next element I want you to think about is your core drivers. These are three core things that are going to have the largest impact on whether you achieve your "how to win" statement. So it could be your service strategy or recruiting for new leaders. It could be developing new menu items to ensure you continue to serve your identified guest avatar. Whatever it is, ensure it's in line with your "how to win" statement. Look for critical elements that will give you the best return on time or results for your business. Remember, stick to three critical drivers.

(We'll revisit both "how to win" statements (or rally cries) and core drivers in Chapter 5, "Are You Playing to Win?". There, we'll unpack them in more detail and you'll see how they contribute to pushing your company to the next level.)

The last element on the tactical side of your one-year plan is core projects. These are all the active projects you've committed to internally or with third-party partners that you are currently working on. For example, you may be redoing your website, creating a new online strategy, designing new menu boards, or implementing new delivery packaging.

Whatever it may be, write it down. Once you have this list of active core projects, rank them in priority order. You have to be brutally honest here. A project may feel absolutely critical, but ask yourself if it's serving your "how to win" statement. Does it need to get completed this year? Is it a priority this quarter? Or can it be suspended? Again, remember the Rule of Three and your promise not to overcommit; you can't do everything. Find those three projects that serve your goal for the year and double down on them.

When I do this exercise with leaders and their teams, listing their core projects usually shows them how much they overcommit

to in a year. A lot of them then have fun with simply killing projects—canceling them to redistribute that time and energy elsewhere. There's a lot of power in that simple process because it reaf-
firms everyone's commitment to the goals that really matter.

So far, you have your "how to win" statement, your core drivers, and the core projects you're going to focus on for the year.
Those are all your strategic goals. But how do you get your people to buy into those goals? How do you make sure they're emotionally aligned and those statements are not just words? More
importantly, how do you keep yourself and your team grounded in
the human values that make your organization great as you work
toward these targets?

Core values are critical here. Every top-performing organization
has core values, so I'm not going to ask you to create some. What
I want you to do, though, is make sure those values are grounded
and alive. They can't just be something you print on a T-shirt and
hand out at conferences. From your organization's list of core values, I want you to pick three that are going to help you hire, fire,
and make critical business decisions in line with your tactical goals
for your one-year plan. These operating values are what will anchor
you and your people as you move through these targets for the year.

The last element of the one-year plan is your commitments.
These are value-based commitments you make when it comes to
the delivery and execution of your one-year plan. Every leader
in the organization who has access to this plan understands that
although they want to deliver a profit target or goal for this year,
they can't lose sight of these commitments.

We usually divide this element into three categories: (1) commitment to your guests, (2) commitment to your people, and (3)

commitment to quality. Commitment to guests could be anything that provides value to the guests walking through your doors. Perhaps: *we're going to have engaging service consistently.* Or: *we're going to create an environment that's a great place for date night.*

The same thing is true for your commitment to your people. Your people show up for you every day; what are the three ways in which you're going to show up for them? Maybe you commit to coaching them or creating a work environment that lets them spend time with their families and friends. Choose whatever is right for your organization. And commitment to quality is simply a commitment to food and beverage quality and quality of service.

That's your one-year plan. All of this is simplicity—not complexity—on a *single* page that allows you to tell a story around the goals that you've set for your business for that year.

YOUR THREE-YEAR PLAN

The Young President Organization (YPO) is a global leadership community of presidents, CEOs, and chief executives. Each year, YPO hosts a global conference where they invite top leaders from around the world to share their thoughts and expertise. At the 2017 conference in Vancouver, British Columbia, they shook up this structure a bit. Instead of asking for keynote speeches, they asked their speakers for their thoughts on how businesses could succeed in the next ten years.

The biggest takeaway from that conference? Fifty percent of businesses won't exist in the next ten years.

We can already see it happening. As you read this, Tesla is on its way to launching self-driving, energy-efficient trucks. What is that going to do to the transportation industry? The same thing is true for the hospitality sector. If you think we'll be unaffected by the future, think again. Just look how COVID-19 has changed us; think about how many restaurants are now involved in delivery compared to the small percentage before.

All this is to say, I don't believe in five-year or ten-year plans. No one knows what the world is going to look like then. What I encourage you to do is make a three-year plan and make sure your vision is in the direction of being viable and relevant for those three years. Focus on a clear and strong delivery strategy that's profitable.

Your three-year plan should be broken down into four quadrants: business, people, guests, and personal.

- **Business**: What does success look like? What do you want to see happen with the business in three years? How much do you want to grow? For example, your goal in the next three years could be that you want to triple your growth or you want to grow 10 percent in your existing stores while opening forty new restaurants.

- **People**: Who do you need in order to support your vision and help lead your businesses to attain your goals? What positions do you need to fill? What does your employee depth chart look like? Do you need to work on staff turnover? You could set a goal, for example, to reduce your staff turnover to 80 percent from 120 percent in three years.

- **Guests**: Who's your ideal guest within this timeframe? Create a specific and focused core guest avatar you're looking to serve. How are you serving that guest and your community?

- **Personal**: What do you want your life to look like inside and outside of work in three years?

I have a personal vision board in this same quadratic format that helps my life outside of work stay on track. (I describe my vision board in more detail in Chapter 11, "Execution-Focused Strategy.") My personal board is broken into four quadrants, some of which echo my business vision board: Personal, Team, Company Operations, and Guest/Community. All four quadrants are in one frame. I add visuals because people remember best through images or vivid stories rather than lines of text; it's what they connect to. I then place this vision board where I can see it: on my phone, taped to my bathroom mirror, and in my office. Seeing it so often and in so many places helps me remain focused on my goals, and keeps me working to achieve them. You might want to do something similar with your three-year plan.

Remember, you don't need tactical goals in your three-year plan; save those for your one-year plan. What you need is the general direction your company is heading in so that you can course-correct if you need to. If we get too tactical or detailed in the three-year plan, you may get bogged down and not complete the exercise.

SHARE YOUR GOALS

How do you engage others in your vision? You share it. You tell stories around it, because people remember rich and vivid stories. Clearly

12-MONTH VISION BOARD | PROFESSIONAL

PERSONAL	TEAM
COMPANY OPERATIONS	GUEST/ COMMUNITY

MATT ROLFE

mattrolfe.com

WESTSHORE
ONLINE

articulating the direction of the business throughout your hiring and training process as well as in ongoing communications with your staff gets them engaged and involved in reaching your goals.

One of the most successful pub operations in North America, in my opinion, is FAB Restaurant Concepts. They have incredibly successful pub restaurants, with great financials and great revenues—they've continued to scale throughout all the challenges we've faced in the restaurant market in the last decade, building out concepts that have become their neighbor's first choice. But a few years ago, they started to lose people. Once you're successful as a multisite restaurant group, people see your success and start to recruit your management. FAB Restaurants decided that what they needed to keep moving from strength to strength was to make a commitment to their people.

It's easy to keep that vision as an intention and overall tagline, but how do you really follow up on it? What FAB Restaurants did—and we worked together with them on this—is holding a series of workshops with their people. In these workshops, they *shared* the intention of the ownership to double down on people. But they also asked for feedback. They talked to their team and said, *What does people development look like to you?*

Then they listened. They listened to what their people wanted for their futures. They listened to what their team needed to buy in and what they wanted in terms of support. And what FAB Restaurants was able to do through these workshops by sharing their goals and through this co-creation process is really cement what their people development strategy looked like. They implemented one-on-one meetings so every manager in the organization could sit down with the person they reported to once a week and discuss where they were versus their goals and how they wanted to develop. That one-on-one meeting was a time commitment FAB Restaurants made to their people. It let them connect with the leaders. It provided them with candid feedback that allowed them to grow. It created opportunity for recognition that didn't exist before.

That's just one example. Here's another: the organization provided its people with financial education. Not only were leaders and managers coached on how to understand a P&L statement, but they were taught how to influence it in order to drive results. That's coaching every one of those leaders would own for the rest of their lives.

By sharing their goal with their team and getting their buy-in, FAB Restaurants didn't just talk about people development; they actually created a strategy and implemented it. The impact was startling. I did a workshop with them just before COVID-19 happened, and the managers were so excited they would have run through a wall for that company.

Without vision and clear plans to execute it, leaders tend to go back to running their restaurants the same way as always: focusing solely on operations, scheduling, managing, and inventory. But without a solid, structured strategy that includes the active development and growth of your people, you're never going to build revenue and expand into multiple outlets. If you expect your staff to spend more time at work than with friends and family, they need to feel connected to the vision and purpose of your business. Tell them what that is and get them invested in it with you.

Time and again, I see great people quitting great businesses because the leader has failed to communicate. I'm not advocating sharing anything overly sensitive but rather stretching your comfort level in how much you reveal to your people to create trust and momentum. If people don't know where you're headed, it's hard for them to imagine what their contribution might be to the success of the business, and they may end up leaving as a result.

A recent buzzword in the hospitality industry is "pivot," but I prefer the term "co-creation." Co-creation means giving your team the opportunity to provide input and feedback on your plans for the business. The people you especially want to hear from are those responsible for executing your ideas inside your restaurants. An exercise that I've found useful for this is "positive and negative patterns." It allows your team to share with you—candidly and constructively—what the business is currently doing that gets a positive result and what the business is doing that no longer delivers a result you want.

Both parts of this exercise are crucial. It's important to know the positive patterns because then everyone is crystal clear about the specific actions they must keep doing to deliver results for your guests, staff, and restaurants. Similarly, knowing what's no longer working gives you a chance to correct it. Overall, the exercise allows the team to be heard and understood, and you can share back with them what you commit to doing based on their feedback. You don't have to change everything because staff gave you feedback, but just by sharing that message of *we heard you and we're going to take action*, you can make a huge impact. It creates significant buy-in from the team, not just at the senior level, but across the restaurants.

I've seen the impact of co-creation with multisite restaurant groups firsthand. We worked with the JOEY Restaurant Group on a project where we emphasized co-creation of the strategy as their

POSITIVE vs. NEGATIVE PATTERNS

POSITIVE PATTERNS

When we do these things consistently,
we get great results

What We Do: Positive Impact

1.

2.

3.

4.

5.

NEGATIVE PATTERNS

When we do these things consistently,
we don't achieve the results desired

What We Do: Negative Impact

1.

2.

3.

4.

5.

mattrolfe.com

primary focus. We ensured that *every* single leader in that company had the opportunity to see the strategy. Add feedback. Offer advice, based on their positions, about how they might achieve their goals, and warn about what might get in the way.

Then together as a group, we shaped the plan. I have *never* seen a team of that scale—we're talking more than a couple of thousand employees—be able to pivot and drive different results. It was exceptional. We started the project because the company was falling off its profit target by a few percentage points thanks to pressure from the market. Because of the co-created strategy, they were able to fix that 3 percent drop in profits and move to a more profitable business model. And that's in some of the most challenging business conditions I've seen.

As Benjamin Franklin once famously said, "Those who fail to plan, plan to fail." A clear plan creates focus and momentum toward accomplishing your goals.

Knowing where you're going is the first step to getting there. But you also need to make sure you have the right people in your organization to help you scale your business and build it out.

How do you find your tribe?

✕

KEY TAKEAWAYS

- When you don't have clarity about who you are and where you're going, your business suffers. To be successful in the hospitality industry, you have to 100 percent know where your business is heading and why.

- Your vision statement offers clarity on where you want the business to go in the future, while your "why" statement outlines why your people should care about your vision.

- Create your one-year plan and three-year plan so that you have a clear roadmap for how to realistically achieve your goals.

- Sharing your goals with your people will encourage their buy-in.

- Where possible, co-create with your team, especially those responsible for executing your ideas inside the restaurant. The "positive and negative patterns" exercise helps you get feedback on your strategies so that you can create realistic goals.

CHAPTER 4

FIND YOUR PEOPLE

"Get the right people on the bus
and in the right seats."

—Jim Collins

At the end of the day, it rarely comes down to the four walls of your restaurant, the chairs, glassware, paintings hanging on the wall, or even your menu. What truly makes a restaurant unique is your people.

Think about it: your competitors can duplicate pretty much everything about your restaurant—the concept, the design, the menu. What they can't recreate is your culture or staff. That's the real differentiator between you and everyone else out there.

High-performing restaurant leaders at high-performing restaurant groups don't do it alone. To reach that level of success, you need to surround yourself with people who support your vision and believe in what you believe. As Seth Godin explains in his book, *Tribes*, a tribe is a group connected by the same vision and leader. Be a great leader to your tribe and watch your results soar.

LET GO

Eric Thomas is one of the top speakers on the planet, and I was lucky enough to attend one of his events. During his presentation, he shared a story. To accelerate the growth of his business, he actually had to step down from being the CEO. Even though he had founded the company and it was his, he realized strategic decisions, proposals, and strategy work were not something he was particularly good at. His unique talent is to motivate, influence, and inspire people. Knowing he'd built a strong team of people, he took himself out of that role and trusted the business would continue to run smoothly with others in charge. He now gets to focus solely on his gifts, and his business continues to grow and thrive.

You already know you can't do it alone. If you're reading this book, then we know you're overworked and short on hours. You might have more tasks on your desk than you can get through. Your calendar is full. And exactly as we saw with Clark Lishman in the Introduction, you're facing a mountain of work you may never be able to climb. This chapter is where we show you how to get through this. Here's where we talk about how you find people who believe what you believe, hire them to support you, delegate responsibility, and move in the direction of your goals and desires. This is where you find your tribe.

But to begin that process, first you have to let go.

Eric Thomas did it. He stepped back from controlling his organization down to the minute details and trusted that it would get to where it needed to go.

I did it too. One of the biggest reasons my company made it through COVID-19 was because I realized I was no longer the best person to be CEO. I'm a perfectionist, and that slowed things down and overcomplicated processes, priorities, and innovation at a time when we needed momentum and velocity. The right decision was to move me to where I'm best—communication, vision, coaching, and strategy—and make space for my partner James to take over as CEO. That made space for James to make faster-paced decisions and for both of us to springboard the company forward, rather than me staying in the same position and being a bottleneck.

I realized my talents were better suited to coaching rather than day-to-day management of my company, and I learned to step back. Was it easy? No. Not at first, anyway. But I knew James was better at management than me, and I trusted him. Once I stepped back, we had three consecutive years of the highest revenue, profitability, and culture scores in the history of the company. If I had held on and continued to do things the same way—a.k.a., trying to do it all—my business would have suffered and I would have lost a trusted collaborator in the process. Since making these changes, we've multiplied our output and even launched another company with great success.

There are many reasons why leaders struggle to let go. Take the time to identify what's holding you back from this step, so you can address it and move on. I recently did a workshop with Ryerson University where I worked with an incredible leader named Jen, who was heading their hospitality, events, and operations. The university was developing and growing its teams, so they brought Jen on to manage these sectors.

When she joined, she planned to let go of operations on the hospitality side. She was handling strategy for the whole organization, so she really wanted to delegate operations to her managers and free up some time. In the many sessions I had with her, she always talked about letting go. But we found that, over the years, there were still tasks she was holding on to. That really affected her managers. They saw it as micromanagement. They saw it as a lack of trust. It impacted them.

So we dug deeper. We used a predictive index and some personality profiling, and what we found is that it wasn't *about* trust. Jen trusted her managers. It was about process. In certain cases, she hadn't fully defined to herself the result she wanted to see or the process to be followed, and so she couldn't fully hand the task over. Once we identified the root cause of Jen's resistance, it was easy to fix. We worked on process execution, explained to managers where Jen's resistance was coming from, and were able to document the process so that both parties could work toward delegating responsibility and balancing expectations. And Jen was able to let go.

Of course, it won't always be process that's holding you back from letting go. Sometimes it is trust—leaders are often frustrated that their people cannot step up and fulfill the responsibilities delegated to them. That fuels a belief that they need to do everything themselves. But in my experience, the bottleneck of growth isn't that managers aren't able to step into their new roles. It's usually that the leader hasn't articulated expectations clearly. They haven't provided any clarity on what they expect to be delivered, executed, and performed by the manager. Of course the manager doesn't meet their expectations—they don't know what they are.

Articulating your expectations is crucial to setting your people up for success and giving them the opportunity to truly step into higher roles. You also need to create *gravity* toward the new role. What I mean by this is you have to create a compelling and exciting force *pulling* your manager into their new role so that they can let go of their old one.

This is best illustrated with an example. One of the most exciting leaders I've worked with was promoted from GM of a $12-million-annual restaurant to Director of Operations. This was a huge promotion for him. But there weren't a lot of clear tasks on his plate as Director of Operations. He would finish his job quickly, and then when he didn't know what to do with his time, he would go back and try and be GM of the restaurant he just left.

This was his comfort zone. He liked being GM; he did it well. He ended up frustrating the *new* GM, who felt he wasn't being allowed to truly take over the job. And so he quit. This leader was getting in the way of someone else doing their job simply because there wasn't enough gravity toward the new role he was stepping into.

We resolved the problem through workshop sessions with the leader. We sat him down and got him to talk through what he was doing with his days, what success looked like, and how he was going to be recognized for it. We got him to identify and acknowledge his behavior as well as the fact that he couldn't be both GM *and* Director of Operations. And then we created a better definition of what success looked like in this new role that was compelling and exciting—as well as how he could measure it—so that he was drawn into his new position and not back into his old one.

Which brings us back to the final bottleneck to letting go, the one most prevalent among top-performing leaders: we don't want our people to fail.

Personally, this is my biggest challenge. My own failures had a significant impact on me, and I didn't want anyone else to experience that pain. So I made it my job to rescue people. To my leaders and my managers, that showed up as not being able to let go. I was micromanaging. If someone on my team had a meeting with a big client, then I would coach them on how to do it. They would make some progress. The client would ask for a proposal. Then I'd come parachuting in and say, *Hey, I have lots of experience proposal writing—let me do that for you.*

I thought I was helping. But here's the reality: I wasn't in the meeting. I didn't have a rapport with the client. I probably didn't even fully understand their needs. All I did was take away a touchdown from the business development manager. I took away their ability to find their own failures and their own wins.

And I didn't realize it until Megan. Megan was hired to take over the business development part of the company from...well, me, essentially. She was hired to be the face of the business with our clients, staff, and industry suppliers. She was an incredible leader. But we had friction, it got bumpy, and she decided to leave. She agreed to do an exit interview with us, which was very gracious of her, and what she said really blew my mind.

She said, *The one thing I wish you did, Matt, was I wish you allowed us to fail. I knew you couldn't because you didn't want us to make the same mistakes as you did, but all you were doing was babying us at every single turn. And that felt like you were puppeteering us into becoming you, which didn't allow us to grow or develop.*

By rescuing us, you stunted our growth. By rescuing us, you slowed things down.

After that interview, I got in touch with a few senior leaders who had worked their way through our company. I asked, *Did I baby you?* And they laughed. They couldn't believe I didn't know it. They said, *Of course you did. If you let us fail more, we could have become our own person on your team.*

It took Megan for me to change. And the first few times I let someone fail, my instinctive reaction was, *I should not have let that occur.* But over time, I realized the benefits of it. When someone failed, we could discuss why they did what they did and what we needed to change. We could decide a path of action that the person agreed with, not just followed. Zig Ziglar, one of my favorite development coaches, always said, "Telling is not selling." I could tell someone what to do all day, but allowing them to fail in a way that didn't significantly impact them or our clients created an experience that accelerated their growth ten times more than my micromanagement could.

I'll leave you with one last example of the power of letting go. Scott Frank is the COO of Craft Beer Market and one of the most talented people I've ever had the privilege to coach. Scott can do everything. His output is double the average leader's. People just expected it of him—that he would put in double the hours and deliver double the results, on top of doing a lot of strategic and tactical thinking for the company. Through our coaching, though, and because Craft Beer Market was expanding into such a huge organization, Scott realized he needed to let go.

One of the first instances of him doing so was for a newly built restaurant in Kelowna, British Columbia. This place was an incredible summer destination—beautiful vineyards, beautiful lake-front, and a massive concept with huge revenues. This was a very important restaurant for the organization, *and* it was about to open. Everything pointed to Scott to do the strategic planning. But Scott knew from our coaching that he needed to let go. So with our help, he created some direction for what the Kelowna location needed to be and then delegated it to one of his regional managers, Franny.

I remember him calling me up soon after he did that, worried. *I don't know if I provided enough direction*, he told me. *Was I clear enough? What if I go there and it's not what I wanted?*

And it was a genuine fear, because if he went there and was disappointed, it would discourage the regional manager who put it together.

But the truth was that Scott had done the right thing. He provided clarity up front, in the form of expectations and some direction for the regional manager, and then he created the *opportunity* for Franny to produce the result.

When he went to Kelowna to see the final result, he called me from the airport on his way home.

Matt, he said, *it's better than anything I could have put together. Of all the plans for my upcoming restaurants, this is the one I'm most excited about.*

Scott's story shows the value of letting go. Once you're clear with your direction, candid about what you want, and willing to get out of the way, those around you can produce something for you that's even better than what you could have produced for yourself.

Be a Scott. It's common for operators to think they *should*— or even that their people expect them to—do everything. But doubting your employees is not the way to encourage ownership or support of your mission and vision. Concentrate on what you do best and leave the rest to the people you've carefully selected for their ability to handle those activities. This is the only way to achieve momentum and velocity toward your goals.

Stop doing and start leading.

IDENTIFY AND BUILD OUT YOUR TRIBE

Success compounds and explodes when you attract the right people to your business—people who believe what you believe. Whether you're opening your doors for the first time or adding people to your management team or seasonal staff, landing top talent is the goal. Clearly communicating your vision, your intention, and who you serve is the first key to building a strong team.

Through some work with Entrepreneurs Organization, I had the opportunity to spend some time with Colin Moore, the Starbucks president at the time. Colin was involved in Starbucks' rapid growth phase—he added 600 stores in his short tenure. He did that by being clear on what allowed Starbucks to scale successfully: their people. He knew exactly the right kind of person to work with their team. And those were people who not only wanted to work at Starbucks because of the benefits and coolness of the job but really *believed* in the experience (as defined by Starbucks CEO Howard Schultz) that Starbucks was looking to deliver to its guests.

In short, find your tribe. Starbucks knew the profile of their ideal employee. They were always on the lookout for what they defined as the captain of the football team or the captain of the cheerleader team—someone who would represent them with energy, engagement, and connection not only within the team but also to their guests. Those are the people you're looking for. Someone who can deliver both your experience internally for your culture *and* the guest experience for those walking into the four walls of your restaurant.

To identify and build out the right tribe for a company, we usually work with the three-step strategy of Attract, Retain, and Develop.

- **Attract:** This is the first stage of putting together a tribe that connects with our company's identity. In this step, we focus on how to find people who believe what we believe and draw them toward our organization so that they apply and interview. It's more than just job postings. It's our belief that we must find the right people who are going to stay with us and help us build out our restaurant group.

- **Retain:** Once we find those right people and get them to join our organization, how do we retain them? As you know, the annual staff turnover for a restaurant is more than 100 percent, so this step is absolutely crucial. What's our strategy for keeping people with us? This could include how we coach them, develop them, or how we provide upward momentum or growth within the organization.

- **Develop:** The last stage is about developing our people. Once we've got them on our team and they see their future with us, how do we develop them into the leaders we want them to be? This step is important if we want to let go as top-performing operators and owners. To do that, we need a committed strategy of investment in the

ATTRACT, RETAIN, DEVELOP

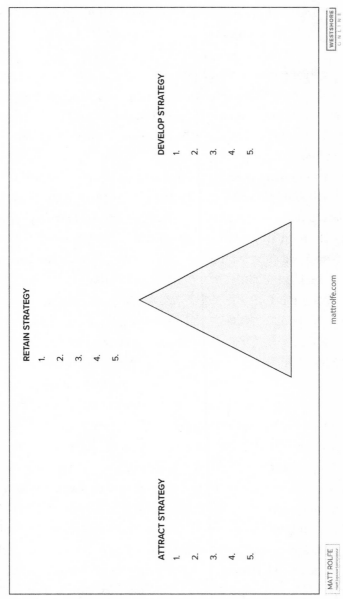

RETAIN STRATEGY

1.
2.
3.
4.
5.

DEVELOP STRATEGY

1.
2.
3.
4.
5.

ATTRACT STRATEGY

1.
2.
3.
4.
5.

mattrolfe.com

MATT ROLFE

WESTSHORE
ONLINE

growth of our people so that they're set up for success and can better support us.

A strong team doesn't just land in your lap. You have to take the steps necessary to recruit, develop, and support their efforts to keep them engaged and employed with your business. Attract, Retain, and Develop is a comprehensive strategy to help you do just that.

Also remember when finding and building your team that talent will only get you so far. People can graduate at the top of their class and go on to mediocrity. The opposite is also true: people can barely graduate and move into greatness. Perhaps a staff member might need to work harder than another, but it's the hard work that makes the difference. Don't overlook that.

We often forget to acknowledge the blood, sweat, and tears—not to mention the time and effort—a millionaire or a pro athlete dedicated to getting to where they are. We only see the success. People don't think about how the man with the yacht worked ninety hours per week to be able to afford that luxury, or how the one with the Lamborghini spent years tinkering in his garage to launch his now best-selling product.

North American motivational speaker, author, and minister Eric Thomas claims his formula for success was his willingness to put in the work. He stopped talking about natural talent a long time ago because success comes from commitment, not just talent. Fight and determination make the difference, so when building your team, be sure to not limit yourself by only looking for talent.

One way to attract the right people to your team—hard-working people who align with your company culture and who will be your cheerleaders—is to craft a good job posting. When coaching clients, I often print five job descriptions with the titles removed: four from their competitors and one from their own business. Many owners are surprised when they can't identify their own, or they select the wrong one. But the reality is, most ads say the same shit: great place to work, awesome team culture, flexible hours.

The biggest mistake you can make in job ads is talking about what *you* want and need as an employer. The approach has to change. It's not about you! So what kind of information should you tell potential employees when advertising job openings? I advise including the following:

- Your commitment to employees and guests
- Your vision for the business
- Your commitment to supporting and developing people
- What's hard and what's rewarding about the job

The most important thing is to present your expectations honestly. Top-performing groups usually ask for things the average operator doesn't. If a manager is going to have to work a seventy-hour week because the goal is to triple your company over the next five years, make sure candidates know that up front.

You have to create this kind of trust and connection from the outset, even with potential employees. Show them something different, honest, and unique about how you communicate the reality of the job. Talk about what it means to work for your business, what type of support is expected from all levels (top, core, bottom), and what everyone is expected to deliver on a daily basis. Get everyone on the same page from the very first moment.

I also encourage you to share the goals of your organization with candidates. If an A player or superstar is joining your team, I can promise you they're going to want to know what progression looks like for them. What's their path to leadership? How you answer determines their buy-in. We'll delve deeper into developing a path to leadership in Chapter 7, "Invest in Your People," but for now, I want you to keep in mind how crucial being *candid* is. Share with your candidates what growth looks like for existing stores or for potential units. Talk them through how, based on that growth, you're looking to develop potential new leaders. That will ensure your candidate is connected to your company's beliefs and vision. It will also show them where they may be going in the future, because no A player wants to join a flat organization.

Matt, you say, *that's not a problem. I'm happy to be as candid as you like in these interviews. My problem is that there just aren't any A players out there. I can't find staff right now.*

You'll be surprised by the number of clients who tell me this—you're not alone. But after working across dozens of great restaurant groups, I can tell you that your problem is not that there aren't great applicants out there or you're not receiving enough applicants. It's that you're not chasing them hard enough to get them to interview with you.

Look, the game has changed. Before, someone would apply and you would call them once. If they didn't call you back, you abandoned them and moved on to the stack of people who would actually come to the interview. But the reality is that now there are more open positions in restaurants than there are people to fill them. And that's true whether we're talking front of house, back of house, or the management team. Your responsibility now is not just to call them once but to try and really get in touch with them. For example, we call every qualified applicant three times. If they've provided a personal number, we text them. We even try through social media.

What helps you keep track of these attempts is an applicant tracker (there's a link at the end of this chapter so you can go and download your own). An applicant tracker is a tool that lets you keep track of your applications. You can check it to see the gaps in your process. So if you received a hundred resumes for the job, who have you reached out to multiple times and who has committed to an interview? I can guarantee that once you start using the applicant tracker, you'll see that your gap is not fewer applicants; it's that you haven't tried hard enough to get in touch with those who would be a good fit.

Chase down your team. Work hard to find the right people to take your company to the next level. It's an investment worth making.

INTERVIEWING EFFECTIVELY

A desperate owner once told me he just needed more warm bodies. That's no way to recruit a high-performing team! This mentality leads to constant turnover and poor performance.

Getting the interview process right is critical because staff turnover is one of the biggest expenses for any restaurant group. Just because it's not measured on most P&Ls doesn't mean it isn't burning a hole in your pocket. Studies estimate that it costs *one to ten times* a person's annual salary to replace them. Let me explain how that breaks down.

If one of your senior leaders quits the organization, you need to spend time and money attracting someone else. Once you have your candidate, you then need to spend time training them and bringing them up to speed. Based on the usual turnover rate in this industry, they're probably going to leave in six to twelve months, and then you have to go through the whole process again. By the time you actually get somebody to stick in that position, you've invested one to ten times their annual salary in finding that person, training them, developing them, and retaining them in their role.

That's the financial impact of rushing an interview.

The best hires happen when you are methodical in your hiring process. I'm a big fan of multi-touch interviewing, especially when it comes to leader and manager positions. You should aim for a minimum of five contacts with a person before you make an offer. By contact, I mean touching base with them, either through calls or interviews.

I know that five contacts sounds like a lot. But I truly believe you don't see a candidate clearly or have them show up in a comfortable way until further along in the interview process. No one shows up to an interview and turns out to be a ten-out-of-ten candidate for your ten-out-of-ten company, so everything's perfect; let's get married. You need time and space to ensure they're a right fit.

Here's how we do it. The first contact is a filtering call, where someone calls the candidate and invites them for an interview. The second contact is a group interview, where we can put them on the spot because they don't have full control of the meeting; it gives us a chance to see a bit more personality. The third contact is an interaction with their direct manager—the person actually hiring them. The fourth contact is with their senior leader or another manager. That gives us multiple approvals of the hire. And the fifth contact

ATTRACTING AND HIRING A PLAYERS

Create a Job Ad → Post a Job Ad → Filter Resumes Received → Attempt to Contact Qualified Candidates 3x to Invite to a Group Interview → Host Group Interview with Key Decision-Makers → Choose Who You Are Hiring → Make the Offer → Candidate Accepts Offer and Is Scheduled for Training

mattrolfe.com

is really just allowing the candidate to come back and make sure they've done their research on us.

You don't have to follow this exact example. Maybe five touch-points is still too many for your organization—if so, pare it down. But make sure you're interacting with the candidate at multiple points in the process because that's what leads to conversations that allow both parties to be seen. And please get rid of any ego that you need to be interviewing *them*. I encourage you to have them interview you as thoroughly as possible; that's how you know they're serious and they understand you from a personality and team perspective.

If the potential hire is someone who may move up in your organization, I also advise employing personality profiles. Some of our clients use Predictive Success or DISC reporting, but there are other options available as well. The purpose of this added step is to determine the candidate's core personality type and how well that might fit in your organization. Based on the cost of a poor hire—which we broke down above—these tests are really worth investing in and have multiple ROIs. We've found these profiles incredibly useful in making the right hires as they help you examine the opportunities, risks, and benefits of potential employees.

But the value of personality profiling goes beyond aligning the candidate with your organization. These tests also show you how they fit into their potential team. A personality profile of a candidate will show you how their personality type *interacts* with other personality types already on the team. This gives fact-based context to your conversations about the hire. If we're hiring for a bar manager role, for example, we'll also get the personality profiles for the existing GM, the AGM, and the night manager. Then we'll evaluate the benefits and risks of adding that candidate to the team.

We ran this test for the leadership team in my company. We weren't looking to hire, but we were curious about our leadership composition and how it influenced the company. We found that everyone on the team, except for me, had the same personality type, one which would prevent them from making quick decisions. Once we became aware of this, we became more conscious of our decision-making process. Once we knew we were going to have challenges making decisions because no one wanted to upset anyone else, we corrected for it.

The last thing you want is to bring someone on board and then six months later find them unmotivated or disappointed in the job. I've met with many managers who were told one thing during the hiring process, but then found the reality of their job to be the exact opposite. They haven't seen their boss in three months, and aren't experiencing anything close to the awesome culture they were sold on.

I've also seen people recruit celebrity chefs by offering a $200,000 salary on top of the $50,000 recruiter fee. Six months later, the famous chef is gone because they were told they'd have greater flexibility and they didn't get it. It hurts everyone and everything when expectations aren't made clear—especially your bottom line.

Turnover is costly and common, but it's not inevitable. Over 60 percent of the workforce is actively looking for other employment—but what you want is a 100 percent engaged and active workforce. Approaching the recruitment process slowly and openly ensures everyone understands and is up for the job.

If you're going to shift your team to success, you need to make sure you have the right people on the bus and in the right seats.

When companies hit the red line and they're at capacity, there's always this panic of, Do we have the wrong people? There's a chance you might. It may be that you have to fire someone who doesn't fit your culture as well as you thought. If that's the case, do it, even if it's difficult to replace them. You'll be better off in the long run taking the time to put the right person in their place.

But 80 percent of the time, we find that when companies push this panic button, they *have* the right people—just in the wrong seats. When you put together your team, you must ask yourself, *Are we putting our people in a position to execute in their core talent?* Because if you haven't, then you may have the right talent, but they're misallocated on what they're responsible for. The ramifications of that could be small—perhaps they're misaligned on their day-to-day responsibilities. But it could also be large, especially when we're talking about senior leadership teams—they could have the wrong project, the wrong role, the wrong team.

Hiring the right people is all about identifying the ones who align with your business. When you find them, that's when the magic happens. Think long term!

CELEBRATING HIRES

While farewell parties do happen, I don't think having people leave your company should be a cause for celebration. I learned this from Jack Daly, who's an incredible and very animated sales coach. (Jack used to say that if he wasn't sweating through his shirt by the end of the presentation, he didn't bring all he could.) Jack pointed out that celebrating people *leaving* is very strange. Celebrating their first day, however—*that* was incredibly important.

I agree! That's why I advise making your employees' first day special—it should certainly be more festive than their last. Integrate them into the positivity of your culture on day one!

At my business, we give every new hire a bottle of Dom Perignon. There will be balloons at their desk and cards from team members. A gift will be waiting for them, as well as a gift for their pet or their significant other. We recognize that it's not just our hire who's joined our team but their family too. We want to make sure the family feels welcomed and recognized—we're grateful that they've *all* made the decision to be here.

One thing I've always found disappointing is when a new hire shows up and their computer is not set up. Their business cards are not printed. Their phone's missing or their uniform is scheduled to come next week. That's a no-go for us. Everything they could want to kick off their employment is at their desk on day one, usually in a shiny box and wrapped in a bow. We want the message to be crystal clear, *We thought of you. We're ready for your arrival.*

We also celebrate our new hires' first day with quality time. Often someone joins a team only to find their manager run off their feet. How often have you heard, *It's great to have you! We're so excited! But shit, I've got to run for a meeting—can you read those manuals and watch that video and I'll get back to you by the end of the day?*

At our company, the senior leader who the new hire reports to spends the day with them. This leader is fully present—they're taking the person through the process, giving them the attention they deserve. Remember, someone's made a life decision to join your company. You want to celebrate that. We then take the new hire out to lunch with more senior leaders; this often includes me.

That way, the person is spending time with not just their direct leader and gets more exposure in the company.

We wrap up the day outside the four walls of the office, where we can all gear down in a more casual setting and the new hire can spend social time with the team.

That's their first day. In their first weeks, we make sure they have time scheduled in their workdays—not their evenings and not their weekends—to read some of the core books we recommend, like *Getting Naked* by Patrick Lencioni. And when they achieve their first goal, we give them a gift. This gift could be champagne or tickets to the theater. Whatever it is, we make sure it's going to interrupt the pattern. We want it to stand out so that when they open that bottle or sit in those front-row seats, they're making a memory they'll never forget.

We've been doing this for ten years now, and I can tell you—people are blown away. Celebrate your employee's first day, and you'll show them how committed you are to their future in your company.

BUILDING YOUR BENCH

Most companies recruit in times of absolute need. But the truth is, top-performing leaders are consistently in pursuit of the right people and constantly working to retain them. You should *always* be recruiting, even when you're not currently hiring. Taking a different approach to finding people gives you greater opportunity to win.

Some businesses even employ depth-charts, just like the Dallas Cowboys team does for their quarterback position. They always have multiple players in their pipeline, and the team has moving, active conversations with these candidates throughout the year.

Investing in your business is more than just having the cash to build it. You have to invest in your team, or they just might bankrupt it faster than you can design a new menu.

If you aren't actively recruiting for leadership positions in your company and someone quits, you have no potential replacements to start wooing. You're stuck and have to start looking for the right person from scratch—which, as we all know, is a long, tedious, and expensive process. You don't want to be forced into hiring from the point of need. Ongoing conversations with potential candidates give you the time and space to select the right person for the job in a timely fashion, no matter what might happen along the way.

Also consider implementing an internal recruiting process. Recruiters may seem expensive because they're an obvious hard cost, but there are a lot of hidden costs to hiring on your own— management time, the cost of the wrong hire, and so on. You might pay a recruiter $50,000 for a placement, but I can promise you that if they were able to find a candidate you currently didn't have access to, this is a great investment that provides a substantial return. I encourage you to keep an active network of recruiters and develop your relationships with them in case you need to fill a position quickly.

SLOWING TURNOVER

A hundred percent annual staff turnover is the industry average. Industry average sucks. And industry average has the opportunity to bankrupt you. Even if you're not at risk of going bankrupt— even if you're the most successful operator reading this book—I still know one of the most heartbreaking times of your year is when a senior leader you *believed* in and you thought was going to be the next staple of your leadership team up and leaves. And you didn't see it coming.

What are the costs of this ongoing cycle? And what's the risk to your operations, especially if you're scaling existing locations?

It's time to make a change. You need people who will stick with your organization and grow with it. The first place to start breaking the wheel is with your own limiting beliefs. Maybe you think you can't find great employees because there aren't any in your city. Maybe you think you are simply unlucky. Maybe there's a "good reason" for each person's departure, and circumstances out of your control determined their decision to leave.

Limiting beliefs run the gamut, but they're never rooted in truth. You must, therefore, change your beliefs to change the cycle.

The reality is you're likely attracting the wrong people. Or you're not investing enough in retaining the people that *are* right for you; you're not developing them. Remember Attract, Retain, and Develop? Focus on that strategy. Put your people first.

If you want to know why you're losing people, the best way to find out is to ask them. Exit interviews are a great way to identify negative patterns in your company. A lot of people say, *Hey, people don't show up to my exit interviews!* (Well then, that's negative pattern number one.) But honestly, to get people to show up to exit interviews, you need to host them in a way that allows people to be candid about why they're leaving. Maybe they didn't see the opportunity for their next position. Maybe their hours weren't what they expected. Maybe the job ad that they applied to was fundamentally different from the job they were hired for. You'd

EMPLOYEE AVATAR

NAME:_____ DEPARTMENT:_____

NAME:_____
1.
2.
3.

NAME:_____
1.
2.
3.

NAME:_____
1.
2.
3.

APPLICANT TRACKER

NAME	POSITION APPLIED FOR	CONTACT #1	CONTACT #2	CONTACT #3	CONTACT MADE Y/N	INTERVIEW INVITE Y/N	ATTENDED INTERVIEW Y/N	ACTION/RESULTS
1.								
2.								
3.								
4.								
5.								

be amazed at what we hear. Whatever it is, put your emotions to the side and listen. Exit interviews are how you learn to be better.

Another way of identifying negative patterns in your company is to ask your current team. What are three things that are working for them in their job today? And what are three things that, if they could change or improve, they would? Those are indicator patterns that you can hear from people *before* they leave. If you can take action to correct these patterns, then the benefits are both financial (you're reducing turnover) and operational (your team isn't disrupted by someone leaving).

Once you've found the best people in the company, hired them, and ensured they're deployed in the right seats, it's time to move toward success. You've now got your key elements in place: vulnerability, clarity, and the right people. But the same trajectory that got you here won't get you to the next stage of your restaurant business. In the next chapter, we'll talk about how you can succeed with these winning elements in place—and it begins with a very important question you need to ask yourself.

✕

KEY TAKEAWAYS

· To begin your journey of finding your tribe, you first have to let go.

· Set clear expectations and gravity in new roles, so that the people who step into them are able to deliver the results you want and give their role the attention it deserves.

- Let your people fail.

- To build a strong team, identify your ideal employee avatar and use the three-step strategy of Attract, Retain, and Develop to draw them toward your company.

- In the battle between talent and hard work, always choose hard work.

- When recruiting, share your expectations honestly with your new hires so they know what is required of them.

- Chase your top talent down! It's no longer enough to call them once and expect them to turn up for an interview.

- Create a methodical, multitouch interview process with at least five touch points or contacts. The cost of turnover is one to ten times a person's salary—that's the cost of rushing an interview!

- It's not enough to just find the right people on the bus; you have to make sure they're in the right seats.

- A consistent and ongoing recruitment process will ensure you're not short of talented people when you need them.

- Recruiters may have a hard cost, but they save you many hidden costs. They're worth their weight in gold.

- Celebrating your people's first days shows that you value their entry into your company and the future they're building with you.

- To reduce turnover, identify negative patterns affecting your staff by holding exit interviews or asking those who work for you.

CHAPTER 5

ARE YOU PLAYING TO WIN?

"What happens when you decide
to go *all in* in life?"

—Gian Paul Gonzales

"Hey Matt, are you open to hearing some honest feedback?"

I hired Colin Collard, a coach who supports entrepreneurs in gaining the clarity they need to grow themselves and their businesses.

"Of course," I responded. It would be a waste not to utilize the expertise I was paying big bucks for, even though I was nervous about what he was about to say.

"Are you playing to win, or are you simply playing not to lose?"

I'll be honest—that was one of the most offensive things anyone has said to me. I don't think I've ever been so triggered in my
life. I didn't respond, but a million thoughts ran through my head.
What does he mean, "playing not to lose"!? I wasn't playing not to
lose! I was working sixty to seventy hours a week. I worked hard to
build a fantastic team. My business was growing—enough so that
I could afford this incredible coach. I was definitely playing to win!
The nerve of this guy!

"You're not playing to win when you're playing it safe," he continued as I sat there in stunned silence. "You aren't pursuing your true
opportunities. You're not stepping into your power and your ability."

What Colin meant is that we were going down the same track
we always followed. We were setting targets that were achievable.
And we weren't stepping into new, challenging opportunities
because we told ourselves we were already too busy. We needed to
push ourselves if we really wanted to play to win.

It took some time to digest what he said. In fact, I initially was
so deflated that Colin compared me to a 200-pound wet blanket.
But I eventually realized he was right.

I was playing not to lose. It's a safe place, but you can't play it
safe in the rowdy restaurant industry. That kind of strategy might
support a business for a short period of time, but if I didn't stay true
to my opportunity and niche in the market and wasn't being true
to myself and my leadership team, I was going to come up average.

And guess what? Average in our industry won't get you to the
next level. I changed my mindset to one of winning instead, and
I've been on a great trajectory ever since. My mindset made all the
difference in the world, and in this chapter, we'll go over what that
looks like so you can work to change your mindset too.

WHAT DOES WINNING LOOK LIKE?

When I coach clients, I share that story to highlight the power of shifting your mindset. There's a huge opportunity in our industry, but to capitalize on it, you have to be clear on how you win. The momentum and focus you bring by defining winning for your business is incredible.

In the Netflix series *The Last Dance*, Michael Jordan holds his first championship trophy like it is his baby. He tears up as he talks about how many years he spent focusing on that trophy and how much he desired it. His depth of conviction is unmistakable. Being as clear on your destination as he was about winning that trophy means you'll be able to take action to attain it.

We host a series of hospitality leadership workshops where we invite leaders from top-performing restaurants and restaurant groups. Our aim is to create a room full of thought leaders who are learning throughout the day but also sharing with each other the ways in which our industry can become stronger. In our last hospitality leadership workshop, one of the sessions I hosted in the afternoon was called "How to Win." And I asked this room full of 175 accomplished, brilliant leaders in the fourth largest market in North America, *Do your people know how you win? Is your GM, manager, and server clear on what success looks like for this year?*

To even *my* surprise, not a single person raised their hand.

I honestly thought some of them would. These were the best in the industry, and I expected some would have done this with their companies. But not a single leader raised their hand. Either they couldn't articulate to themselves what their company's winning statement for the year was, or they didn't believe that if they called up their GM, their manager, or one of their servers, that person would be able to repeat it on the phone.

After that question, we started talking about what the impact would be if everyone knew what success looked like in their organization. The point wasn't to shame anyone for not having done this but to anchor these leaders in just how great their companies were, asking, *What if we made a slight pivot and focused for the next thirty days on making sure our people knew how we defined success?*

I can tell you, the energy in that room *shifted*. There was a buzz you couldn't control. We went on break afterward, and usually people are sluggish on breaks, but here they were making calls, talking animatedly, writing down ideas. And when everyone came back to the sessions, we actually had to take a minute to calm the room down.

That's the power of articulating what success looks like to you. The leaders in that room knew the impact it would have on their organization if they got this right. They sensed it. The reason sports are so exciting, entertaining, and frustrating at times is that the team and the fans know what success looks like, and they know when they aren't attaining it. When high-performing restaurant groups are structured to win, you get more fans and better ratings. People support your brand and buy into your vision.

That's exactly what happened with FAB Restaurants. FAB Restaurants are independent brands within a group of pubs, and they set their definition of winning as, "we want to be our neighbor's first choice." They were neighborhood pubs, so they had to be clear on how to measure this definition in terms of the service experience they would create. Being a neighborhood pub is fundamentally different from, say, being a restaurant that serves the masses in movie theaters. You're serving people *through* the restaurant. If you want to become your neighbors' first choice, you have to create connection. You have to know them, understand them—invite them to return.

So they set about defining tactically and strategically what "neighbor's first choice" looked like. And they focused on the *benefit*. The benefit for the guest was a better experience. A better experience usually leads to higher check average. Higher check average usually leads to more tips. But what it also helped FAB Restaurants articulate is that their winning statement will lead to guests returning to the restaurant more, creating this positive cycle of that experience. And when they implemented it, that's exactly what they saw. But articulating it beforehand helped them get that buy-in from the business, the staff, and the guests—exactly as sports teams do with their fans.

DEVELOPING YOUR RALLY CRY

So, how will you know you're winning? And are you playing to win the championship or just get through the season? Like Michael Jordan or LeBron James, you need to have passion and conviction for what winning looks like.

You'll need to determine your core focus—or, as I like to call it, your rally cry. You've encountered this concept before, in your one-year plan (Chapter 3); here's where we'll dig into how that simple statement can really impact your business.

Most people, when I ask them to create a rally cry, say, *We already have a vision statement, Matt.* That's great, but that's not a rally cry. A vision statement is for longer periods of time; it's what you put down in your three-year plan or when you're thinking about the company's growth across the years. But a rally cry—while it might be connected to your vision statement strategically or through language—is the single most important goal your business has *now*. It is your core focus for the year.

Do you remember Pizza Nova's Welcome, Wow, Ciao? We talked about it in Chapter 3. Welcome, Wow, Ciao was Pizza Nova's vision statement. It was what they needed to get right with their suppliers, their guests, and their franchisees. It was their goal for the long term. Their *rally* cry in the year that they introduced Welcome, Wow, Ciao, however, was "all in." What that rally cry meant was if they didn't have everybody in their organization buy into Welcome, Wow, Ciao—if everyone wasn't "all in" when it came to achieving that vision statement—then they didn't have a chance to scale and provide that experience to their guests. So their immediate focus was for their people—from the delivery driver to the president—to go all in to make sure they achieved Welcome, Wow, Ciao.

A vision statement is your longer-term goal, while your rally cry is a tighter and more tactical statement toward that longer-term vision.

When composing your rally cry, remember that it's for your whole organization, not for an individual or a department. Keep it short: a simple statement of one or two sentences that everyone can remember. Make sure it fits with your culture and is easily measurable so everyone always knows if you're on track or not. Avoid the temptation of borrowing someone else's rally cry just because they're in the same industry. It's theirs because it fits their business, and it may not fit yours.

Pay special attention to the language of your rally cry. We once created a rally cry of "Supporting the Middle." By middle, we meant the middle of the organization—your mid-level management and people working in restaurants. The concept was good. But when we rolled out the rally cry across the organization, it failed. No one wants to be middles. The language made the middle management feel judged, so they resisted the rally cry.

We changed it to "Supporting the Core," and there was instant buy-in. "Core," of course, is the most essential part of your organization, and the language made people feel valued. So don't underestimate how language can make or break your definition of success.

If you take the time to get your rally cry right, it can catalyze your organization. One of the most powerful examples of a rally cry that I've seen in action was with a client of mine, a large-format racetrack and casino. Anyone who's been to a casino on the gaming side or visited a horseracing track will know that there are a very dominant set of regulars. These regulars are rowdy, they're focused, and they're absorbed in what they're doing.

My client's regulars had a huge emotional imprint on the staff. Every time someone from the staff approached one of these regulars, they were snubbed. People lashed out at them. (It's a casino; tempers run high.) And so the staff began to create a narrative. *Everyone's horseracing or gambling, and they don't want to be disturbed. Sometimes they've lost, sometimes they've won, but either way, they're emotional and they're frustrated. All they want is for us to leave them alone.*

So that's what the staff did.

The reality of the situation was that a very small percentage of guests were regulars—essentially, people gaming so hard that they didn't want to be disturbed. But the staff wasn't interacting with *anyone*. To fix this, we stepped in and created a rally cry: Make

Every Experience a Winning One. Based on that definition of success, we began asking the right questions. Who are the client's different core guests? How do we identify them? What would be *their* winning experience and how would we deliver it?

By rewiring the focus with our rally cry, we got the staff to slowly buy in. We identified a core guest avatar that was comfortable and safe. Staff would go to them and make passionate recommendations for new food items. They would recommend new buffets. They would approach these guests for drinks more frequently. And over time, we were able to prove to the staff that they're not going to have a negative reaction with everyone and people *did* want to be approached. We changed their perception.

It created a better experience not only for the staff, but also for the guests, who got a significantly better service experience. Tips went up. Gaming went up. And the business boomed.

COMMUNICATING YOUR RALLY CRY

As we've discussed in Chapter 3, clarity is power. Leaders need to have a clear definition of success. The clearer your goals, the more momentum and alignment you can create in reaching them.

If you're not clearly communicating what success looks like, there will be no momentum behind your goals. They need to be front and center, all the time. A one-time message isn't going to cut it. You can have an entire corporation fired up at a kick-off meeting, but if that's the only time you talk about your goals, you will lose traction.

It's like a vision board. Every strategy meeting, weekly meeting, and leadership meeting should begin with talking about what kind of traction you're gaining toward your rally cry.

Here's how we roll out the rally cry in our business. We hold an annual conference where we make sure the rally cry is delivered in an exciting and interactive way. You need good delivery to get a message to stick with people—stories matter. When our leaders announce the rally cry, they don't just say it. They provide examples of when we have taken similar actions to achieve similar results.

For example, if our rally cry is "get it done," we describe times in the past when we've been able to push on difficult goals and get it done. This creates trust and buy-in from our people; it shows them that the rally cry is not a stretch goal. It says, *We've done this before; we just need to do it more consistently.*

Once you've rolled out the rally cry, have your district managers hold a follow-up conversation with their people about it. These managers talk to their GMs and chefs about what the rally cry looks like for the set of districts and regions they lead to reinforce the intention, purpose, and importance of the rally cry. At the end of that conversation, district managers ask their venue managers to share the rally cry with the location team.

There are several benefits to this process. First, you're repeating the rally cry several times throughout the organization so people are more exposed to it. Second, you're giving your management at all levels the chance to truly understand the language of the rally cry. It's one thing to grasp the concept. But what we want is the rally cry to *live* and *be alive* inside the restaurants. For that to happen, your GMs and chefs have to fully own it. By allowing them to present it, you ensure they can get behind it completely.

Of course, your rollout plan can't end there. It's crucial to repeat your rally cry at every opportunity so that it's always at the top of everyone's mind. We stick our rally cry at the beginning of all our meeting agendas. And we create a scoreboard.

A scoreboard is a tracker of simple key metrics that shows where we are in relation to our goals. You know those billboards you get on highways? Those billboards are designed so that you can read them in three seconds as you drive past. A scoreboard is like that. Its purpose is to show at a quick glance whether you're winning or losing versus your rally cry or core focus. We post our scoreboards where everyone can see them, whether that's online or physically in all our locations. It keeps the conversation focused on what matters most. Are we winning? What did we do to win and how can we do more of it? If we're losing, how can we course-correct?

ESTABLISHING YOUR THREE CORE DRIVERS

Once you've established your rally cry based on your most important goal, it's time to determine the three core drivers that will help you achieve your overarching goal if you consistently focus on them.

You've worked on your core drivers before, in your one-year plan (Chapter 3, "On Vision: Clarity Is Power") so you'll know that these need to be tactical and measurable. Everyone needs to see if you're on or off track at the end of the first week of the year, the twenty-sixth week, and the fifty-first week.

Delivery strategy, guest experience, and employee development are all examples of core drivers. For each of the core drivers, you want to define *three* ways to deliver on that driver.

For example, say you're looking to deliver the core driver of guest service, which is how you interact with your guests. The reason "guest service" is a core driver is because it's measurable, but what are the three ways in which you can measure and achieve it? List those down. You could measure it through increases in check average. You could evaluate online shopper reviews. And you could set up a mystery shopper to go experience the guest service delivery in your restaurants and report back to you.

If "delivery" is your core driver, then three ways you might deliver on this could be improved packaging strategy, making unboxing sexier, and providing better food quality.

ASSIGNING OWNERSHIP

The next step is to determine which person, department, or team owns each driver. Using the example of employee development, you might determine:

- Managers are required to have a three-hour training session with employees every three months.
- Leadership will meet with each leader or manager on a biweekly basis.
- The CEO will share feedback from mystery guest shoppers each quarter, celebrating wins and offering feedback for improvement.

One thing I want to get clear here is the difference between accountability and responsibility. In my experience, there's often a lot of gray areas between the two, and clients can be confused about who to look to when it comes to driving results. Being clear on who's accountable and who's responsible is key to achieving your core drivers.

When we talk about accountability, we mean the person whose job it is to deliver the results. This is the person who gets rewarded and recognized if the result is delivered and who is held accountable if it fails. Get clear on that one person who is holding the bag, so to speak, so there's no finger-pointing if the results aren't achieved.

When we talk about responsibility, however, we mean the team or people responsible for *helping* deliver the result. So the person who is accountable for a core driver won't actually be doing all the work themself. They'll have a team that's responsible for putting in the work to achieve the core driver. It's important for the person accountable to coach, support, and lead that team so that they're able to make progress toward the committed goal.

People development is now becoming the norm in the hospitality industry, and great leaders recognize how important it is for reaching business goals. Decide how often you'll pull people together, the workshops you're going to develop and present, and if you'll offer external coaching. Above all, be clear on who plays what role in delivering a core driver—whether they're accountable or responsible—to make sure you have a clear idea of ownership of the goal.

RECOGNIZE PROGRESS

It might feel a little like you're standing on one side of the Grand Canyon right now, and the goal is to get to the other side. You're excited about putting all this to work in your business but don't know what the first, second, and third steps look like. How do you cross the chasm?

The answer has to do with why most New Year's resolutions are abandoned within twenty-one days. Someone might resolve to lose ten pounds, lose four pounds in three weeks, and then quit. Why? Even though that's solid progress, without clear steps to success and ways to see progress as it is happening, a goal may seem unattainable.

To get all the way to your goal—to cross the Grand Canyon—determine what progress in the direction of your goals looks like. You need to know where you are, where you want to go, what you haven't yet measured that still needs to be measured, and how long each step of the process should take. Figure out what behaviors will best contribute to achieving the results you're seeking.

I once worked with a top national restaurant chain that consistently achieved their goals but had no idea how they were doing it. There was swagger and sexiness to the group—their leaders were young; they were consistently achieving double-digit growth. They just had no idea how. Was it their marketing? Restaurant design? Service delivery? At their scale, they couldn't identify the cause. And although they were one of the top-performing groups in North America, their fear was that if they didn't know what they were doing right, they couldn't replicate the pattern. If one year their profits fell from 12 percent to 6 percent, their team would have no choice but to focus on the negative (that fall) because no one knew what the positive was (what they were doing right before).

They hired me to get clarity as to what behaviors were driving their achievement. We changed how they measured their goals. We shortened the measurement period from annual to quarterly. Instead of getting to the end of the year and checking if they achieved their double-digit sales growth, we set targets for each quarter on what we were going to focus on: service focuses, costs focuses, and people focuses. And then we tracked interactions and behaviors to see what they were doing that created a positive or negative trend. Reporting on that scale allowed us to narrow down the results, and we successfully identified what was giving them that stellar double-digit growth.

THE POWER OF ROUTINE

Now that you have your core drivers and you know who is accountable and responsible for them, it's time to make sure they're implemented across your organization to deliver results. And here's where I face the most resistance. I've given keynote presentations to rooms of twenty to two hundred people, and the main pushback I always get is, *I'm already maxed out. Where am I going to find time for this?*

This is an important concern, especially for your core staff. Consider your managers for a moment. Leadership sets goals and puts pressure on managers to make those goals happen on the front line—that a certain dish will be plated or beverages presented a certain way. Often, those same managers then get pushback from their teams in dining rooms and kitchens that takes the form of, *Don't you know…?* Don't you know we're short-staffed, don't you know we don't have time, and so on.

It is incumbent that leadership support the core. That includes creating space for them when you set new goals. It includes giving them permission to say "no" to other things as priorities change.

As your "core," they're in the middle of everything: daily operations, caring for guest and staff needs, and executing strategy from leadership. They're held accountable when it comes to delivery in every aspect of your business, and they feel pressure from all sides. They're overstretched. If they're assigned to deliver your core drivers, they don't know where they're going to get the time to achieve the results you want. How are they meant to focus on rally cries and core drivers when they're holding everything together?

To fix this, I take them through an exercise I call the "eight-to-thirteen concept."

In this exercise, I ask them to identify the top three tasks that, if they did them consistently in their roles, would allow them to deliver on their new goals. Say you have a core driver of "guest service." What are the top three things a manager can do in their specific role to deliver on this core driver? They could be, for example:

- How, and how quickly, you should greet your guest.
- The expectation for providing passionate recommendations.
- The process and timing for checking in and offering "another round."

Once they have these three things, I ask them, *If you were to spend an optimal amount of time on each task, how long would it take you in the week?*

I've taken thousands of people through this exercise in different workshops, and by the time we get clear on the optimal amount of time to spend on each of these three areas, it fits into eight to thirteen hours of their week.

This is actually crucial to breaking down their resistance. When a lot of managers hear about new strategies, they think they need to spend *all* of their time implementing them. They think it needs to dominate the week. That's overwhelming, and that *is* impossible.

But eight to thirteen hours in the week is far more doable—to them, the goal begins to look a bit more realistic.

But we take it one step further. Remember, these are managers who are already overstretched; they've started this exercise with a full week. So when we settle on these eight to thirteen hours and I begin to work with them to schedule it into their calendars, I give them permission to take out something else. They're not *adding* those eight to thirteen hours to their week; they're fitting it into the hours they already work.

If you're reading this and thinking, *Great, what do they possibly take out?* don't worry—we talk about a time audit in the next chapter, which will help you and your people reorganize their schedules to drive the results you want. For now, I want you to focus on giving your core managers and your people the permission to *make space* for the strategies you're implementing. Often these strategies are created in a boardroom, and by the time they're introduced to a role at the store level, we're not taking into account everything that a leader already has on their plate. We're not giving them permission to *focus* on those new strategies.

Give them that permission. If you find they need to spend six hours a week working on your attraction strategy, have them put it on their calendar. If they need to spend three hours a week driving profits, that goes on the calendar too. Otherwise, they'll open their calendars with tears in their eyes, feeling there is no way they can meet the goals you've established.

When I run this exercise with people, I get them to surrender to the fact that they don't have *more* hours in the week. There are, after all, only so many hours in the day. But if they just focus and schedule those eight to thirteen hours into their week—an hour or two a day—they'll be able to fundamentally change the results for the business. Then they can spend the rest of their thirty, forty, fifty hours focusing on operations, emails—I don't care, as long as they invest the agreed upon and ideal amount of time in the direction of their goals.

This is how you create space and time to win. First, you break down your people's resistance to the assigned drivers by showing them they won't take sixty hours of their week but only eight to thirteen. Then you give them permission to focus on those new strategies by allowing them to take out something else in their calendars.

There's nothing more powerful than taking control over your calendar and going from serving everyone else to serving your business. You're in the service industry, true, but focusing on the core of your organization is what moves the business forward. Give your people the same space, and you'll avoid unnecessary turnover and burnout.

Once you give your managers time to focus on their assigned drivers, there's no need to track or micromanage them. You already know they're capable of managing a high-performing restaurant, so trust them with this part of the process as well.

CELEBRATING THE WIN

The industry has a history of focusing on what people *didn't* do, where we messed up, and what we can do better. Maybe your team served 300 tables well but experienced challenges with five. At the end of the night, instead of celebrating the 300 excellent tables, the problem tables take center stage and take up the majority of the discussion.

We need to change that. You're more likely to reach your goals if you reinforce behavior that produces a positive result rather than focusing on the gaps. If you want to see more great behavior, you need to recognize great behavior when it happens. Most people are so focused on what they don't have or haven't yet achieved that they never take time to celebrate the wins. They just move on to the next one.

I'm here to advocate for taking the time to stop and celebrate. After focusing on your rally cry, drivers, and goals for so long, everyone in your organization deserves some recognition when you've finally reached them. You want the team to know that you've won and you appreciate everything it took to get there, despite any minor hiccups.

If you want more positive behavior to become a habit, you need to recognize and celebrate it as it happens. Celebrating can be as easy as taking a few moments in a meeting and acknowledging the win. Recognize a person, the team, the project goal, or the deliverable for the quarter. Show appreciation for the effort and the work put in to achieve the result. There's a physical reaction that occurs when people are openly recognized. When people are appreciated, they are more likely to continue putting their best foot forward. A consistently implemented recognition program is the most powerful way to gain momentum toward your goals.

I once worked with a company whose operations team put in a lot of effort to gather together their franchisees and hold these beautiful celebratory dinners for them. This operations group was close-knit; they'd been together for decades. I asked the group, *When's the last time this team took the time to step back and celebrate?*

There was silence. Someone said, half-laughing, *I think we went to a baseball game in 1985.*

It was meant to be a joke, but it wasn't funny. It sank in for the team in that moment just how little they'd celebrated themselves. Everyone was silent. I walked around the room and I said, *That's just not acceptable. You can see the disconnect it's causing. You need to change that.*

We thought a bit about what would have the biggest impact on the team and decided it was food. Everyone on the team loved food. And so when they achieved their quarterly targets for the month, they held a barbecue. They held it right there, in the office. They brought burgers and hot dogs, and someone set up a grill in the parking lot. It was a Big Green Egg (if you have a Green Egg, you'll know what I'm talking about), and it was the only thing the team talked about that whole time.

The point wasn't the barbecue, the Big Green Egg, or what budget was spent—it was to give the team a chance to celebrate themselves and connect through that celebration. It was about taking the time to celebrate their hard work and success.

The bottom line: top-performing leaders find ways to recognize their team. Often this recognition can be low-cost to the company or even free and still have an incredible return. It's just another way to invest in your people, decrease turnover, and increase employee satisfaction.

SHIFTING INTO HIGH GEAR

Right now, you might be thinking, *There's no way we can do this, Matt. This is the restaurant business. We can't do our work based on specific timeframes.* My reply to that is this: always addressing what seems urgent in the moment actually robs your organization of its potential. Staying in a reactive mode is often the biggest roadblock to success.

Execution has to become your new mindset, belief, and part of your culture. If you're truly playing to win, you need to (1) define what success looks like for your business, (2) communicate it to your team through your rally cry, (3) establish the core actions and core drivers needed to manifest that success, (4) assign people to be accountable and responsible for those actions, (5) create time and space to win using the "eight to thirteen" concept, and finally, (6) celebrate your wins. That's the proactive process you need to make sure you're not playing "not to lose." If you shift your mindset to make this happen, you'll shift your results into high gear.

In the coming chapters, we'll talk a bit about what you need to do to equip your people with the tools to deliver on this vision of success. It begins with candid communication. To get the best from your people, they need to know where your company stands—and, more importantly, they need to know where *they* stand in your company.

✕

KEY TAKEAWAYS

- Playing to win is not the same as playing not to lose.

- All top-performing businesses and sports teams know what success looks like for them. Define your version of success by creating your rally cry.

- The language of your rally cry matters; it must be phrased such that everyone in your organization can get behind it.

- If you're not clearly communicating what success looks like, there's no power behind your goals. Consistently communicate your rally cry throughout the year so that it is at the top of your people's minds.

- Your core drivers are what help you achieve your rally cry.

- Accountability and responsibility are not the same. Assign ownership to each core driver, but keep that distinction in mind!

- The "eight to thirteen" concept helps your team make time to execute your core drivers and goals. This is how you create space and time to win.

- Don't just focus on the losses—celebrate the wins!

CHAPTER 6

CANDID COMMUNICATION

"Lack of candor blocks smart ideas, fast
action, and good people contribution—all
the stuff they've got. It's a killer."

—Jack Welch

If you're a leader in any industry, then you've probably heard of
Jack Welch. Jack Welch—a.k.a. "Neutron Jack," the top CEO of
the last century. I grew up reading many of his books. So when I
got a chance to hear him speak, I grabbed it with both hands.

Jack was an older gentleman by then; he'd flown in on his pri-
vate jet and they'd paid him a quarter of a million dollars to be on
that stage. The former CEO of General Electric didn't present slides
or make a speech. He simply sat down and said, *Ask me questions.*

Someone asked about his famous nickname, Neutron Jack. Is it true that he went into General Electric and essentially *blew* up divisions, *fired* staff on scale, and shut down departments, all for the P&L statement?

He said, *That was never the case.*

I still remember the real story, told in his beautiful Boston accent. At every talk that Jack did, he got asked the same question: how did he become Neutron Jack? It's a story that changed over the years, until the real story got lost. What really happened is that General Electric and he decided that if they weren't number one or number two in any industry where they competed, they were going to shut that division down. If they weren't going to be the best at something, then they could reallocate those resources in areas where they *could* be the best.

But Jack was certain not to let go of employees without them being aware.

Your job as a leader is to make sure that everybody knows exactly where they stand, he said at that talk. *If you fire somebody and they don't see it coming, that's your biggest failure as a leader.*

I almost fell off my chair when I heard that because I wasn't doing it as a leader or a coach.

To keep employees aware of where they stood, Jack implemented a plan in which the top 20 percent of every team got highly recognized and rewarded financially. The middle 60 percent got told that they were in the middle: they had to take care not to fall to the bottom, but they also had an excellent chance of climbing to the top. And the bottom 20 percent were told that if they were in the bottom 20 percent for two months, in the third month, they'd be gone. Chances were that if they were in the bottom 20 percent for two months, they weren't the right fit for the organization.

We didn't just let people go, Jack said. *We let every single person who worked for that organization know exactly where they stood.*

I can tell you from the bottom of my heart—having watched people I've let go, my best friends, cry in front of me, shocked because I hadn't been candid or clear enough—*listen* to Jack. Tell your people where they stand. In this chapter, we'll cover how communicating consistently, openly, and honestly at both the corporate and individual level is the way you play to win.

COMMUNICATING WITH THE COMPANY

A major difference I see between average-performing restaurant groups and high performers is their communication. For top companies, clear, consistent, frequent communication is the norm. Time and again, I hear how much people appreciate candid and clear messaging about where the company stands, where the team stands, and where they stand.

It may seem like spending more time on communication isn't worth it. After all, you're already maxed out. But committing to your optimal communication strategy now means you'll spend far less time fighting fires, having hard conversations, and shifting focus. It actually gives you more time to execute your plan to win.

You *must* find the time to communicate more.

To make the time, I recommend you do a time audit. This is a topline audit of where your time is going, and we do it with all leaders when we first start coaching them. This may seem like a brutal exercise, but it's actually one of the most productive things you can do as a leader. Two years ago, I did it and I found that I was wasting 50 percent of my time on unfocused activities that were routine.

Here's how it works. We look at your role and figure out the top five to ten things you allocate your time to each week. At the end of the day, we ask that you take five minutes to reflect and check where your time was invested. Did you complete the meetings you had scheduled? Did you stick to your thinking time—or, in Stephen Covey's terms, your quadrant two time—that is on development and growth opportunities? Did you have flex time in your day? (Most of our leaders have their calendars scheduled in back-to-back blocks, so there is usually very little flex time; we recommend 30 percent to 50 percent flex time, depending on the position.) If you did have flex time, how did you use it?

Leaders usually run this audit for two weeks—some do it for four—and what we're able to learn at the end of those weeks is (1) where you're getting productive time in your month and (2) where you're investing time in projects or conversations that aren't going to move your business forward. This visibility allows us to make critical business decisions on how you can reshape your time to get the best output. That output might be getting to your kid's soccer game. It might be getting to your tennis match. It might be making sure that you've got the right hours to show up properly and communicate candidly with your team.

I've seen the benefits of a time audit over and over again with my clients. There was one client who was working six and a half days a week for *years*. This client had an open-door policy. Anytime he was in the office, his door was open, and during office hours, his phone was on. Everyone was free to reach out to him anytime they needed him.

TIME AUDIT CHECKLIST

KEY FOCUSES AND TASKS What are your focused/desired intentions or outcomes?	MONDAY		TUESDAY		WEDNESDAY	
	TARGET	ACTUAL	TARGET	ACTUAL	TARGET	ACTUAL
Week 1 1. 2. 3. 4. 5.						
Week 2 1. 2. 3. 4. 5.						

mattrolfe.com

TIME AUDIT CHECKLIST | CONTINUED

	THURSDAY		FRIDAY		DID YOU ACHIEVE YOUR IDEAL OUTCOME? WHY/WHY NOT?
	TARGET	ACTUAL	TARGET	ACTUAL	
Week 1 1. 2. 3. 4. 5.					
Week 2 1. 2. 3. 4. 5.					

But it meant that he was always at the service of someone else's urgency. When we did his time audit, I asked him to track how much time he spent in conversation with other leaders and people inside his company. At the end of his time audit, we found that some weeks it was 40 percent and some weeks it was north of 65 *percent*. We didn't change the "open door, phone on" policy, but we did create rules and respect around it. No senior leader can afford to spend 65 percent of their workweek being at the service of others. Your team wants to talk with you, true, but they also want you to *lead*. We taught people how to prepare when they're coming up to talk to him and interrupt his flow. As a result, he began saving time *and* having more quality conversations. He was also able to protect an additional five to fifteen hours a week, which for him, gets him home, gets him to his family, and gets him focused on the vision of the company.

A time audit will help you see where you can make time in the week to communicate candidly and consistently with your people. Don't worry about over-communication. Many leaders worry that over-communication will be seen as micromanagement, but it's actually a key strategy in all high-performing teams. Your job is to keep people's energy moving in the direction of your goals, so you need to keep communicating what these are consistently. I recommend daily messaging—and at a minimum, weekly messaging— to ensure your people don't lose focus on what matters most.

COMMITTING TO CONSISTENCY

The ultimate goal is for everyone inside the organization to be 100 percent clear on what you want them to do and how to effect the most change. Many leaders, however, are unsure of how exactly to create a communication strategy that will achieve this.

No matter what your personal style of communication is, the most important thing is keeping the message consistent. All too often, leaders come back from an off-site retreat with a new plan or project and start to share it enthusiastically with the rest of the team. But over the coming days, weeks, and months, the strategy fades away. After a few too many times of this happening, you've created an expectation that the latest initiative will disappear as well. So why should the team bother getting excited about it in the first place?

The key is proving to the team you're dedicated to staying the course—that the message you're sending now won't pivot, change direction, or add other focuses down the line. Make sure people know you're committed to continuing to drive the goals you're talking about today and won't abandon them for the next shiny new thing that comes along tomorrow. Be clear that your priorities will not shift and you will stand strong.

I had the opportunity to work with Steve Pelton of the Landing Group, who is one of the most successful operators I know. Steve came to me because their business was scaling up; they were moving from their three stores to more locations, and he wanted to make sure that they kept the same sexiness—that *energy* and buzz—that they had when their partners could be in the restaurants for most of the operating hours.

We identified their secret sauce, so to speak—the elements that created a great culture for their people and a superb guest experience that made their guests want to come back. That secret sauce came down to two things. First, they really understood their guest avatar. They had identified their three core guest types for each location (it differed slightly per location) and knew what they wanted and needed. They had then trained their staff on exactly who the guest avatar was and what they would desire so that the staff knew how to meet the guests' needs. Second, they created a simple three-step process on what they were looking to do consistently with *every* single guest that walked in the door. And they made sure they communicated that process to each staff member—manager, busboy, cook, chef, and bartender—so that they could measure it and deliver it.

It was clear that as long as the avatar and guest service experience was executed consistently in their new locations—as long as they made sure their staff knew how to do these two things—they could scale successfully. Steve and his partners did this flawlessly, and shortly after our coaching, they were bought by Cara Restaurants (now known as Recipe) and have been expanded across Canada as a concept.

BEING AN OPEN BOOK

Jack Stack talks about open-book management in his book, *The Great Game of Business*. By sharing the critical metrics and financials in your organization, you'll create clarity, alignment, and understanding. I coach this same type of philosophy with my clients and even utilize it in my own business.

Now I know a lot of operators who are happy to share key metrics but don't necessarily want to share P&Ls or financials. To them, those are confidential. Those days have passed. Your staff is counting your tills. They have an idea of your sales. They see you pull up in that nice car. I *guarantee* you they think you're making more revenue and profit than you actually are. You'll gain far more from opening up those statements to your team than from keeping them closed. Giving them this kind of transparency often results in a reality check that can go a long way in making everyone truly feel like they are in it together.

In my company, every salaried person has access to our P&L sheet, salaries, metrics, and results. That further connects employees to our vision and enhances buy-in. In my experience, taking an "open book" approach gets everyone on board with what we're looking to achieve.

The more you can share fact-based numbers with people inside the organization, the better. Sharing business metrics, targets, and financials enhances engagement with your staff. Without seeing the numbers, it's much harder for people to relate to the goals you're setting for them. As an operator, you should be communicating to your team *what* behaviors create these financial results—this clarifies cause and effect for them. For instance, delivering the ideal guest experience (behavior) leads to an increase in average check amount (financial result). Or keeping an action-focused inventory (behavior) leads to an achievement of the company's COGs, which adds up to more profit (financial result).

A good example of leveraging an open book policy to motivate your staff is Kit Andrew's story. Kit was my first business partner. When he and I first got together to start coaching, he was running a series of nightclubs called Nashville North. This club was full. You couldn't fit any more people into the physical space; it was already queued up around the corner with people trying to get in. But you *could* make more money. All these young kids in the club had wads of cash they wanted to spend at the bar, and they were waving those wads at the staff—but because the staff was focused on the wrong areas, that cash was never making it into the till.

We coached Kit's staff across a series of sessions. We created a set of metrics and financial targets, broken down by bar outlet. At the beginning of each night, we put up a scoreboard of what our financial target for the night for that outlet was. We also shared with the team whether that target was achieved or not.

Through that process, we were able to prove to the staff that extra revenue created tips. They were able to see that result for themselves. Kit and I then came up with a simple calculation we shared with his people: if we were able to achieve the targets we set, each employee could take themself and a significant other to Mexico or on a beach vacation *just based on the extra tips they earned in a two-month period*. That created incredible motivation for them to work toward the targets.

Overall, the strategy was a success. By openly posting financial targets and results that weren't stretch but were simply an indication of what was possible, we were able to see increases in sales of 20 percent or more on already wildly successful bar nights.

CREATING ALIGNMENT

Leaders need to be aligned when communicating. One might say something in a *slightly* different manner than another, and the result is the message sounds *very* different to the marketing team than the operations team. This can create confusion throughout the company. I had a client once who was measuring customer service. I sat down with three leaders in a room, and we created the metric, the process, and the expectation for this. When I came back next month to evaluate what progress we had made, I found that all three leaders had completely different understandings of what the metric meant. Bottom line: pay attention to the language of your goals and be aligned on the meaning of the deliverables you expect. You can't leave it up to assumption or personal interpretation.

That's why it's so important for the senior leadership team to be clear about the overall strategy, messaging, and methods of delivery before anything goes out to the company. This is where the true opportunity in a communication strategy exists. Forcing clarity on how and when to communicate and to whom often ensures everyone in the business is hearing the same message no matter which leader is delivering it.

I encourage every leadership team, whether it's a management team inside a restaurant or an ownership group or board of directors, to wrap up their meetings around a concept called cascading communication. Cascading communication essentially asks leaders to take a few moments when everyone is still in the same room to decide what is going to be communicated, to whom, and by when. Most importantly, *how* is it going to be communicated?

The medium of communication matters. The one thing I find when coaching some young leaders is that they might leave a strategic meeting and choose to deliver the goals and strategies developed through text message. Or they might send an email. And we all know there's a strong opportunity to misunderstand a text or an email. If it's a simple message, text and email are fine. But if it's a critical message, then you want it to be communicated via video call, and you should make sure everyone in the meeting knows that this is the chosen medium of communication so they all use it.

In this cascading communication exercise, I also encourage you to talk about what isn't to be shared. It's not about keeping things confidential as much as it's about not sharing something that isn't *firm* yet. If you share with your people a half-formed idea or strategy that was discussed in the meeting, then they may take it to be a fact. But the reality is it hasn't been fully developed or decided as of yet. And when it's not delivered on, it can break trust.

As I've said before, strategy creation is easy, but strategy execution is hard. As a leader, you need to determine what this looks like and exactly who needs to do what and when. The focus should be on making whatever you're communicating a reality rather than just setting goals, talking about them inconsistently, and then wondering why you're not achieving what you set out to do. Define the effort, focus, and commitment needed—and from whom—to make it all happen.

COMMUNICATING WITH INDIVIDUALS

Everyone needs to know how they can best contribute to the success of the business. The only way to do this is through open, honest, frequent communication. You owe it to your team to let them know where they stand. Candid feedback grounded in positive recognition is the only way to grow your team. It establishes an understanding that you'll consistently communicate about the direction of the business and its success and invest in the development of your people.

Failure to do this can cause heartbreak. I was once witness to backstage conversations between senior leaders about a long-standing employee—someone who had been with them for decades. They were discussing whether this person should be promoted into a newly created role. Their direct leader had their back;

they wanted this person to get the job, and they felt the company needed them. But the senior leader in the organization was convinced the employee was never going to be ready. They were not going to get the job today—they were not going to get the job *ever*. At some point, the trust had broken down with this person, and so the senior leader believed that yes, this person was great in their position, but they were not going to advance. The senior leader was going to let them die on the vine or quit of their own accord. It was a dramatic failure in communication.

The problem was this was a backstage conversation. And all the while, the employee in question was literally pulling their hair out. They even called me and said, *I've done everything I can do for the organization. I've worked weekends, nights, extra projects. This new role's at play. Other people are interviewing. It's my role. Why am I not being considered?*

What the leadership should have done is told this person they were not being considered for the promotion. They should have been upfront about the conflict. Instead, the situation caused a rift in senior leadership, and a critical employee who invested over a decade of their life in the company was getting increasingly frustrated, to the point where they were considering exiting the organization. All because they weren't being told—in Jack Welch's terms—where they stood.

The employee finally left the company for another group that was perfect for them, but these stories don't always have happy endings. Sometimes people stay and the situation gets worse and worse. Only honesty can fix a situation like that. As leaders, we need to stop handing out participation trophies and patting everyone on the back regardless of their performance. Someone who is doing a poor job needs to know that's the case just as much as someone putting in top performance.

The core problem in many organizations is a lack of communication between leaders, managers, and staff. Spending more time honestly communicating with your people now means less time spent re-staffing and scrambling around later.

SETTING EXPECTATIONS

You first want to make sure everybody across the organization—from top leadership down to the newest employee—knows what the company goals are and what is expected of them. They should understand what your rally cry and core drivers are, how these came to be, and why achieving these goals will have a positive impact on guests as well as the individual's location, the team they directly work for, and themself as an employee. Decide whether this comes through an email, text message, phone call, weekly meeting, or one-on-one meeting. Then determine how you're going to check back in to make sure the message was retained and understood.

A company that communicates its expectations really well is Pizza Nova. They had a strong structure before I began coaching with them, but they've added layers to it since. Pizza Nova disseminates expectations through annual calendar plans. They begin with a mid-year franchisee conference, which is a full-day workshop focused on where the organization is; what their priorities, visions, and goals are; and what's expected of what they call "the support office" (for the franchisees) for the coming year. One hundred and fifty franchisees attend this workshop, and what they hear is not, *Here's what you need to do, but instead, Here's what we are signing up to do for you this coming year.* That creates huge buy-in.

The organization follows that meeting with quarterly two-day offsites for their different teams (exec, ops, call center, etc.). They also continue to bring their franchisees together quarterly to drive the conversation forward, workshop it, and make sure they're working on their goals. They *then* have monthly senior leadership meetings, executive team meetings, and department meetings where they get tactical and strategic about their goals.

Pizza Nova's system is one of the best, most well-rounded systems of communicating expectations that I know. This consistent setting of expectations up front and then driving conversation around it ensures that everyone is laser-focused on their goals throughout the calendar year. Better still, it's been proven to deliver remarkable growth for decades.

Setting expectations is important not just for driving your company toward your goals but also for framing what you want out of your managers and employees. Without this piece, they could end up thinking they're supposed to deliver something else, leaving you disappointed in their performance without just cause. That can lead to severe heartbreak on the employees' side, especially when they've been working their asses off to deliver their best.

Nothing upsets me more than seeing this disconnect between a leader and their team. Last year, I had just begun engaging with a client and was running a strategy session for their operations team. We'd started building some trust with each other. Midway through the session, a senior leader came in and just started laying into the team. He was absolutely disappointed with their performance. He was frustrated with how some of the things were done in the company. I respected what he shared with the team.

Then we took a break and I was pulled into the hallway by four people who had just been laid into at the meeting for what they *didn't* do. I could see tears in two of the people's eyes. One of them was red-faced. To them, it felt like the senior leader had no idea what they were doing to keep this business moving forward—the sacrifices they'd made and the hours they were working. And I could see the disconnect. All of it was because clear expectations weren't set and the team and senior leader weren't communicating clearly with each other. Neither of them was spending energy in the direction of their goals. Instead, it was being spent on disappointment, frustration, and anger.

This may seem like a dramatic example, but I promise you it happens on most teams. In the end, we were able to resolve it. I scrapped the schedule for the rest of the day, and we spent some time in that prickly feeling, working through it. But it shouldn't have happened. And when it does happen, teams are often busy ignoring it so they can move on with their agenda. They tell themselves it's a manager or staff issue. But it's not. It's a communication issue. Tony Robbins calls this concept "the value chain." You need to communicate expectations along with any gaps between performance and expectations. If this isn't happening, you're creating a break in the chain and getting in the way of achieving business goals as a result.

RECOGNIZING HIGH PERFORMERS

Most of the time, the business teams that get the most attention are the ones that underperform—the staff member who continuously shows up late and doesn't have their uniform on correctly or the cook who doesn't plate their meals correctly.

In sports and high-performing businesses, however, the focus is the opposite: top performers get all the attention. As a leader, I believe you should be having fewer conversations with bottom performers and more with your best ones. Fixing what's broken isn't the key to success—accelerating and multiplying your effort into what's working is.

Recognizing people who are doing great things results in them leading from the front. They'll pull the middle of your organization to a new, higher standard, and your bottom performers will leave because they don't fit into the culture anymore. The person in the back who's always talking smack and taking cigarette breaks will quit because their complaining no longer gets the attention that it once did. Focusing on top performers moves your culture forward.

Recognition is always intended and often thought of but not communicated. And that's because of how busy we are and the pace of the hospitality industry. Taking all this into account, recognition should be a process.

That means it's not genuine! you're thinking. *It's not spontaneous if we planned it.*

I can promise you it is genuine; we're just making sure we share it. By making it a process, I mean you should know who you're going to recognize for what and by when and what your budget is. How large the budget is doesn't matter! I don't give a shit. All I care about is: have you spent your budget? Because if you haven't, then that means that you or the leadership team didn't give this the attention it deserved.

I also recommend tracking recognition points. Recognition points are basically about who we recognized yesterday or last

RECOGNITION AND CELEBRATION PRACTICES

	WHO DID YOU RECOGNIZE?	WHAT DID YOU RECOGNIZE THEM FOR?	HOW DID YOU RECOGNIZE THEM?	HOW DID THEY REACT?	HOW DID RECOGNIZING SOMEONE MAKE YOU FEEL?
1.					
2.					
3.					
4.					
5.					

week or last month, and for what. If you collect enough of these points, you can start compiling them into what I call a "best practice guide." It will show your team the behavior you plan to reward in your organization. And that will have a ripple effect because when your staff starts following these behaviors consistently, it creates the best service experiences for your guests. Those guests then return. They tip more. Your staff gets happier and works harder to implement those behaviors. It perpetuates a positive cycle, and it all starts with recognition.

"RESETTING" WITH POOR PERFORMERS

If you're a leader wondering why people aren't performing to your expectations but you're just sitting in your office allowing the behavior to continue, it's not your staff's fault. It's your fault. Unacceptable or below-standard performance that isn't corrected becomes the new standard. It doesn't matter if the underperforming employees have been with you for ten days, ten months, or ten years—the behavior sticks and spreads.

That's why you can't let poor performance snowball. I know it can be nerve-wracking and awkward to tell a manager they aren't meeting goals or expectations—so much so, you might even avoid having a conversation about it at all. You might justify your inaction by citing other challenges that need to be tackled or not wanting to risk the manager leaving and creating a bigger hole in the business. But the outcome of avoidance is that the poor performance continues. And guess what? By that point, you're now at least half of the problem.

What I recommend in this case is called a "reset." Resetting requires you to first admit your contribution to the situation, be vulnerable, and share from your perspective. I advise structuring your reset conversation in this manner:

- **Acknowledge your role.** Explain that the business hasn't been hitting its targets, partially because you haven't been coaching the way you should. Maybe you haven't been passionate enough, or you haven't brought many suggestions to the table. Tell the manager you realize you should have communicated this earlier.

- **State the problem.** Present the results and current position of business goals, repeating behavior, engagement, and so on without judgment. Promise to better guide the manager in the future, and assure them you are committed to recognizing and reinforcing when they're producing the right results.

- **Give them space.** After sharing negative feedback, give the manager some time to process what you've said. They'll need to decompress. I recommend a timeframe of forty-eight hours or less.

- **Check in and move forward.** After they've had some space, check back in with them. Ask if they're also willing to surrender the past and move forward. Tell them you are willing to start with a clean slate. You really have to mean this fully. Don't tell someone you're going to give them another shot when you're really waiting for this next mistake. Surrender, trust, and reevaluate.

The days of focusing on what's broken are over. Don't use a reset to ask for new behavior and then wait for the person to screw up again. In order for conversations like this to be successful, you have to surrender first. You can't change the past, but you can admit your part in it and vow to co-create a better future with your manager.

Write down the desired outcome before having a reset conversation or meeting so you can focus on it and avoid getting derailed by emotion during your talk. In addition, make sure you don't enter into a conversation like this with too much energy. Assess your physical and mental state. If you're amped up, angry, or frustrated, wait to talk until after you've calmed down.

Candid communication with your team is crucial if you want to play to win. Clearly state your company's goals, express your expectations up front, and tell your people where they stand. If you do this, you will support them to blossom in their roles and give you their best.

In the next chapter, we'll talk about how you can develop your people to *outgrow* their roles and become the leaders you need as you scale your business. People development happens by design, and we'll talk about how you can put a plan in place.

✂

KEY TAKEAWAYS

- Candid and consistent communication is key if you're playing to win. Make time for it.

- A time audit shows you where you're getting productive time in your month and where you're investing time in projects or conversations that aren't going to move your business forward.

- Your messaging should stay consistent—it should not pivot, change direction, or add other focuses down the line.

- An open book policy increases buy-in from your team and helps them work more efficiently toward your goals. This means sharing KPIs, directives, and financials—yes, financials!—with your people.

- Make sure your senior leaders align on the language of your messaging as well as what will be shared with whom, by when, and how. Spend some time at the end of each meeting on cascading communication, a strategy that ensures you get this right.

- Always be honest with your people on where they stand. Failure to be candid can lead to heartbreak.

- Setting expectations is important, not just for driving your company toward your goals but also for framing what you want out of your managers and employees. Develop a detailed rollout strategy to make sure everyone in the company—from top leadership down to the newest employee—knows what is expected of them.

- True recognition is a process. Take this seriously, and recognize your high performers.

- Recognition points can be used to create a "best practice guide" that will show your staff the type of behavior you want and reward in your organization.

- "Reset" with poor performers to make sure you're not focusing on what's broken but on what can be fixed.

CHAPTER 7

INVEST IN YOUR PEOPLE

"Train people well enough so they leave,
treat them well enough so they don't want to."
—Sir Richard Branson

was having drinks with the senior leaders of the JOEY restaurant group in the Fairmont Pacific Rim hotel, looking out at the ocean and the mountains, when the incoming president leaned in with a question.

Now that you've had a chance to look behind the curtain, he said to me, *what are you most scared of for us?*

I was working with the group on leadership development, and I was really glad he asked the question. It is a great question. This was early into my coaching career, so we had just started to notice critical patterns in the growth of multisite restaurant groups. The JOEY Restaurant Group is an incredibly well-funded group. When it came to scaling up, money wasn't an issue, finding real estate wasn't an issue, and their existing team was absolutely fantastic. They also were one of the fifty best-managed companies in Canada, with an amazing culture.

But the average runway it took for someone starting with the company to go from manager to GM was about ten years.

That was my concern. I said to the president, *Do you have the core people in the company today that, as the organization grows, can support your growth?* What I meant is: was there a bar manager, a night manager, a cook, or a day manager who could advance up through the company to ensure that the business could fill the leadership gaps as they opened more restaurants?

I wish more people would ask me this question because it's absolutely an answer they need to hear. You *cannot* grow a successful group if the majority of your hires are coming from outside the company. That's the biggest mistake groups make; they look for their talent elsewhere. Then a year from now, you've got four people sitting in that boardroom out of a table of twelve who *don't* know your vision, *don't* know your values, and *haven't* seen the company build its way to where it is now—and it creates conflict. There's crisis, at a critical growth stage, about who you are and who you have become. This, in my experience, is the number one factor for implosion.

You must be committed to promoting people from within. These people know your values and your vision. They've proven themselves and their commitment to your organization. They are your next leaders. But to get them to a stage where they *can* lead to support your growth, you have to invest in their development.

This foundation of developing leaders who believe in your vision and have shown their commitment to your organization is what we'll cover in this chapter. It is an absolutely essential foundation for a successful restaurant group. Next to financial rewards, the thing people want most from their jobs is the opportunity to advance their careers. Once they can pay their rent or mortgage, go out for dinner, and live the lifestyle they're used to, they're looking for the ability to grow as a person and develop within their role. If you're not offering this, your employees will leave you for someone who will.

And that development needs to be for *all* roles in the company. In the hospitality industry, there are usually solid plans in place for senior leadership but not for anyone else. There's almost no roadmap in the business if a supervisor or key holder today is interested in running your multimillion-dollar operation a few years down the road. I want you to ask yourself, *What would the impact on my organization be if I started to focus on developing the core or future of my company with intent and commitment?*

I can give you the answer in one word. Astronomical.

FINDING A FRAMEWORK

Most operators in the industry report that they coach their leaders. In the last few years, there's been an increasing trend to invest in people development because businesses have understood that that's what helps you attract leaders, retain leaders and develop a well-rounded culture. Organizations now allocate time for one-on-one meetings, team meetings, and one-on-one development conversations and plans.

That's *great*. I applaud all the businesses that have set aside time to invest in this. But, more often than not, these restaurant groups have made an assumption that their leaders *know* how to coach. And that isn't the case. Coaching is a learned skill. What ends up happening in all these allocated meetings when the leader doesn't know how to coach is that they revert back to what they know. They turn these development meetings into tactical management meetings. They ask about their managers' weekends. And that defeats the purpose of why these meetings were set up in the first place. Worse, it frustrates your people. Imagine going into a meeting to talk about how you plan to develop in your career and instead listening to what you didn't do over the last month that was part of your tactical targets. It's exasperating.

We'll talk a bit more about coaching as a learned skill (and how you can learn it) in the next chapter. For now, what you need to take away is that you need a framework—a structured direction, context, and process—for your people development strategy. You have to give your leaders a philosophy and system to follow. Without a framework, what they call coaching might actually just be an aimless conversation.

Answer these questions honestly: Is your coaching process getting you the results you want? Are you developing people at the pace that you need to? Are you seeing the retention numbers or engagement results your goals require? If not, there's opportunity for improvement.

All the great coaches of our time—Phil Jackson and John Wooden, for example—have a set philosophy they follow to get incredible results from their players. If you want a championship team like theirs, you'll first need to get clear on the process for development

1:1 DEVELOPMENT SESSION
The "7 questions" exercise comes from *The Coaching Habit* by Michael Bungay Stanier

IT'S YOUR TIME! THIS IS ABOUT YOU, NOT ME...	
1. FOLLOW UP ON PREVIOUS WEEK	**2. WHAT'S ON YOUR MIND?**
1. 2. 3.	*The kick-start question helps break the ice.*
3. AND WHAT ELSE?	**4. WHAT'S THE REAL CHALLENGE HERE?**
The awe question generates new opportunities while overcoming the urge to give premature advice.	*The focus question allows you to identify the underlying question or issue.*
5. WHAT DO YOU WANT?	**6. HOW CAN I HELP?**
The foundation question provides a safe space to express what they want, which will help improve communication.	*The focus question allows you to identify the underlying question or issue.*

IF YOU'RE SAYING YES TO THIS, WHAT ARE YOU SAYING NO TO?
The strategic question gets the person to consider if they are all in or if they are only going to commit to this decision half-heartedly.

WHAT IS MOST USEFUL TO YOU?
The learning question allows you to create a moment to coach for development, which will help solve the problem and increase performance.

in your company. Just because you're doing workshops, staff trainings, or webinars doesn't mean you're working on development. Don't mistake activity for achievement, as Coach Wooden preaches.

Even if you've introduced a structured coaching strategy in the past, it's good practice to revisit it on a regular basis. Given the turnover rates in the industry, the leadership team delivering on your development plan today may look very different than the one that was trained in delivering it. Without training or support, people tend to do what they're comfortable with—which may not match your development program at all.

Find out what's happening consistently within your teams or inside of your locations and what has fallen away by asking your core leaders. I recommend doing this through discovery calls, connecting with people across the company confidentially to learn the reality of your current development program. Are conversations happening? Are they happening at the appropriate frequency? Are they following the agenda? That way, you can know your true current situation, what (if anything) needs to be redesigned or changed, and who might need a refresher on your framework.

DEVELOPING A PATH TO LEADERSHIP

Something I work on with all my clients is outlining the path to leadership. You can either have top-performing leaders in your company today, *or* you can hire one in a junior position. If you're hiring one in a junior position, then you're looking at developing that person *through* the company—advancing role by role—into the top-performing leadership role that they could one day occupy. That's what I call the path to leadership. For me, the path to leadership would start with your senior hourly positions and move all the way through to support office, head office, or possibly the operations team outside of the restaurant.

Outlining the path to leadership means understanding how your junior hire is going to progress up the ranks and what they need to do to continually advance through the organization. You should be as detailed as possible when thinking about this. I recommend creating a flowchart like the one below, which starts with the core hourly positions and then works its way up through every position in the management team. For each position, outline:

- What the position is
- The average amount of time spent in each position
- The core responsibilities of the person in that position
- The skills required for that position
- What they need to do or achieve to be considered—not guaranteed but *considered*—for advancement

Then, communicate the path clearly, in an upfront and honest manner, to all of your employees. The earlier you can do this, the more successful your hiring, training, and coaching programs will be.

I know this looks detailed, but trust me—it's invaluable. If you've hired a young superstar, then I can *guarantee* you the first thing they're going to want to know is how they can get to the next stage. Without a detailed path to leadership, you're not going to be able to set clear expectations for them and that's going to lead to heartbreak. If you have a junior leader on your team now who wants to get a GM role inside of twelve months and that's going to take them twelve years, I'd rather they know now before you invest in them.

PATH TO LEADERSHIP

SR HOURLY Average amount of time in this position: _____months	SUPERVISOR Average amount of time in this position: _____months	DAY MANAGER Average amount of time in this position: _____months
KEY RESPONSIBILITIES: 1. 2. 3.	KEY RESPONSIBILITIES: 1. 2. 3.	KEY RESPONSIBILITIES: 1. 2. 3.
CORE SKILLS: 1. 2. 3.	CORE SKILLS: 1. 2. 3.	CORE SKILLS: 1. 2. 3.
HOW THEY WIN/ HOW THEY WILL BE MEASURED: 1. 2. 3.	HOW THEY WIN/ HOW THEY WILL BE MEASURED: 1. 2. 3.	HOW THEY WIN/ HOW THEY WILL BE MEASURED: 1. 2. 3.

PATH TO LEADERSHIP

NIGHT MANAGER Average amount of time in this position: _____months	ASSISTANT GENERAL MANAGER Average amount of time in this position: _____months	GENERAL MANAGER Average amount of time in this position: _____months
KEY RESPONSIBILITIES: 1. 2. 3.	**KEY RESPONSIBILITIES:** 1. 2. 3.	**KEY RESPONSIBILITIES:** 1. 2. 3.
CORE SKILLS: 1. 2. 3.	**CORE SKILLS:** 1. 2. 3.	**CORE SKILLS:** 1. 2. 3.
HOW THEY WIN/ HOW THEY WILL BE MEASURED: 1. 2. 3.	**HOW THEY WIN/ HOW THEY WILL BE MEASURED:** 1. 2. 3.	**HOW THEY WIN/ HOW THEY WILL BE MEASURED:** 1. 2. 3.

If you're hiring someone into a night manager position and their expectation is they're going to progress at a certain rate but that's not what happens in your company, it's much better to tell them in the interview process, *before* you hire them. A path to leadership grounds expectations for your managers that are in place now, and it also sets realistic expectations for those being hired into your team. We need this framework so that everyone is in alignment and on the same page.

Without this framework, you have misalignment and opportunities to break trust. And that's not just between you and your junior hires, but also between members of your senior leadership team. If one leader says, *I think Sally's ready to move up the ladder* and another says, *Sally's not ready. How can she be? She's only been in this role for six months*—then that creates friction. Worse, who does that hurt more than Sally? Here's a person who's ready to move to the next step, and she's being held back by someone who wants to hold her in the job—and can, because there's no clearly defined process, guidance, or framework for the path to leadership. You may have spent years developing Sally in her role, but now she's going to jump ship because she wants to move quicker than your company allows.

Don't lose your investment in great people. Define your path and then let everyone know what that is.

DELIVERING ON DEVELOPMENT

There are many different formats you can use to provide these development opportunities. I like to take a wheel-and-spoke approach. At the center of the wheel is your intention and outcome for your program, and the spokes are what you need to have in place to support it. There's no one-size-fits-all plan, but some suggestions include:

- **Group meetings.** Larger group meetings help refocus people on business goals, how the company is progressing toward them, and what their contribution toward those goals might be. They also allow for senior leadership to interact with developing leaders and assess their growth.

- **Peer connection.** Peer connection is one of the most valuable accelerators there is in business. The majority of industries have peer communities, and I believe hospitality should follow suit. This can happen live or virtually. For example, you might have your GMs across all locations connect on a regular basis to share best practices and vulnerable experiences and to build connection and momentum.

- **One-to-one communication.** Ideally, current leaders should spend 20 to 40 percent of their time each week coaching developing leaders. This should happen on a reoccurring, regular frequency. I recommend scheduling these types of meetings either weekly or biweekly.

- **Effective mentorship.** Many companies set up mentor–mentee relationships the wrong way. They believe the mentee will somehow suck all the wisdom and insight out of the mentor. Those usually don't deliver what they could. The right way is to create mentee-led mentorships. The mentee holds the responsibility to schedule the meetings, to have an agenda, and to come with questions, setting the mentor up to respond effectively.

- **Online training.** In our new COVID-19 era, people are more accustomed to learning online these days than ever before. Although I am a huge proponent of live trainings, there are various subjects—like core expectations—that can be relayed effectively through a video posted to your YouTube channel or company app. To track and manage your online efforts, you can include absorption testing and analytics to see how well people understand your message and how quickly they absorb it. My company, for example, provides staff training through a virtual training site called Lightspeed, which helps us determine metrics about employee retention and comprehension of the material.

I also want you to make sure you're giving your leaders permission to develop themselves during the workweek. I find that a lot of companies ask their leaders to do, say, six hours of development work in a week, but these leader's calendars are already overflowing, so they end up trying to cram it in at two o'clock in the morning after they just closed the restaurant. You don't want that. If you push them harder than they're already being pushed, they may be physically present but mentally checked out. Worse, they may burn out. Create space and time in the workweek for your programs and their developmental goals. It shows the leader that you deeply believe in leadership development, to the point where you're willing to take them off the floor or block off time in their schedules so that they can do the development work.

If you're a committed and progressing leader reading this, then I want you to understand that this development work is also about *you*. It's not just about your employers. It's to develop you as a person, so I encourage passion and flexibility to develop yourself outside of work hours. It could be something as simple as listening to a podcast on the way to work or committing to reading five pages a day, but put in the investment.

As an operator, if you've tweaked your current strategy or recently developed a new one, you may find it doesn't work for everybody on your existing team. Cultures grow, shift, and develop over time, and not everybody will be in alignment with that. The biggest mistake I see in business on both sides—the leadership and ownership side and the management side working for them— is when both sides know there is no longer a fit, but they don't allow the person to move on to new employment. I'll often sit down with a leadership team and find them circling around a person they know no longer fits their role or isn't set up for advancement in the company—that person is stuck and they aren't going to move forward.

I ask these leaders a simple question, *What do you expect from this person in the next month so they can prove to you that they're performing in their current role and that they're set up for advancement in the future?*

I ask that question because it's important to try and support your employees that don't fit your culture at first. Everyone deserves a fair shot. But often, I'll come back to those meetings and what I'll find is that there's nothing that can be done. It's a cultural mismatch or the person doesn't share the company's values. And *that's* a different matter altogether. If someone doesn't share your values, it's a huge warning sign; the longer you hold on to the person, the bigger the separation usually becomes. The impact of this is not on the company, leader, or person who does not fit. The impact is on those who believe what you believe and then stand back and watch you allow someone who clearly does not fit play on the team and, in many cases, negatively impact your culture and results.

If this is the case, let the person go. As long as you do what's right for the business, the people who believe in your vision and your direction will stay with you—and it's better for the ones who don't to leave sooner rather than later.

Once you've created a people development program, there needs to be commitment for it throughout your organization. It has to start at the top and cascade down from there. Once it is communicated to your teams, there's a set and measurable expectation for leaders to deliver on.

Developing your people is foundational if you want to become a top-performing restaurant group, but you can't implement it properly if your leaders don't know how to coach. In the next chapter, we'll delve a bit more into coaching as a learned skill and how to deploy it consistently throughout your organization to multiply engagement and impact. If you build a team of coaches, you'll create a competitive point of difference other companies can't match.

✖

KEY TAKEAWAYS

- Ask yourself: do you have the core people in your company today that, as the organization grows, can support your growth?

- You cannot grow a successful group if the majority of your hires is coming from outside the company. A people development strategy is essential to grow the people in your team—the ones who understand your values and who have proven their commitment—into becoming your next leaders.

- Implement a strategy or framework for development meetings so that your leaders know how to coach and don't turn a development meeting into another managerial meeting.

- A path to leadership keeps everyone in alignment and sets realistic expectations for those looking to progress through your company.

- Not having a path to leadership creates opportunities for misalignment and can lead to heartbreak.

- There are different formats to deliver on your development opportunities. I prefer a wheel and spokes approach.

- You don't have to develop everyone—don't be afraid to let people go if they no longer fit the vision and values of your company.

CHAPTER 8

COACHING IS A LEARNED SKILL

"Tell less and ask more. Your advice
is not as good as you think it is."
—Michael Bungay Stanier

I n the last chapter, we talked about how important it is to develop your people *through* your organization to become leaders, and what that pathway to development may look like. In this chapter, I want to go deeper into an assumption most operators make when they implement their development programs. They believe everyone knows how to coach.

But coaching isn't an intrinsic skill. It isn't obvious; it isn't easy. It's a learned skill. It takes time to develop and execute, and it needs a strategy and approach to ground it. Coaching is not a management meeting wrapped around ops, goals, targets, or daily job expectations. It's not about tactics or KPIs, either. It's about being there and supporting the leader you're looking to grow and develop. Everyone in the company needs to know exactly where they stand, what they're great at, and what their development opportunities are. Through your coaching frequency and process, you'll support them in their growth.

In this chapter, I'll talk you through the elements you need to effectively create and implement a coaching strategy. We'll cover the many parts of a good coaching strategy, who to develop, and what your coaching timelines should be.

CREATING A COACHING STRATEGY

When it comes to developing a coaching strategy, the one thing I always repeat to my clients is *Lift from where you stand*. It's important that you meet the team or leader where they're at. You don't want to develop a strategy that's too rigid or complex for where the group is starting from, but you also don't want to launch a process that's too simple. People will get bored with it and there won't be any buy-in. What you need to do is evaluate where you are. What does your current coaching strategy do? How is it working? Who is engaging with it across the company? And most importantly, is it driving the impact of results that you desire?

Once you have your answers, it'll help you find the right place to start your coaching program. You can then lift from where you stand! Remember, if you're developing across your organization, then that's a significant time investment that adds up to significant dollars for your company. You want to get your coaching strategy right. And of course, once you create that strategy, it's fluid. You can add to it. You'll be lifting from where you stand the first year you do this, and then in your second year, with proper reflection and evaluation, you'll be able to add layers to your strategy as you continue to invest the time.

Once you've evaluated your old coaching strategy and have a clear idea of how complex or simple your plan should be, it's important to set down the frequency of the coaching sessions—and then stay consistent with it! This really is the key to success. I recommend meeting on a weekly, biweekly, or monthly basis, depending on what works best for your company or team. (Quarterly or annual conversations are called reviews, not ongoing development.) We'll delve a bit more into meeting rhythm in Chapter 9, so you have a clear structure for how to consistently communicate with your team and build on their development.

The important thing is to stay committed to this schedule you've set down. The most frustrating thing for the person being developed is having their coach cancel or reschedule meetings. I've found it takes a minimum of a hundred days before your staff really starts to buy in, engage in the process, and believe you're actually committed to delivering on it. Canceling meetings can severely set you back in this process. Make sure you're not over-committing your time and that you continue to make coaching a priority even when the business is at its busiest.

What you coach will depend on where your company currently is and where it's looking to go. What do your leaders need to know? What skills do they need to support your business as you grow to the next level? If the company is rapidly scaling, your coaching needs to focus on having up-and-coming employees ready to successfully lead your new restaurants. If your company is not currently in a growth mode, your coaching might focus less on development, promotion, and advancement and more on making sure your current and upcoming leaders know exactly how to succeed in their position. This is especially important for Gen Z and Gen Y leaders, who have been taught to want what's next. They're not afraid to transition to another company quickly like previous generations were.

Which brings us to a crucial aspect of your coaching strategy: the actual coaching conversations. This is where most businesses assume their leaders are already equipped to succeed and forget that coaching is a learned skill. It's the source of most of the frustration with the process, where managers find they're simply being pulled into a tactical meeting under a different name and leaders can't understand why they aren't seeing the results they want.

What you need are conversations that are focused on the *person*, not on their role or position. The moment you focus more on the role or position, it becomes a management meeting, not a development session. You want the person being coached to drive the conversation to focus on what's important to them. It's then up to the leader/coach to open up, listen, and be present for that person in the room.

The biggest failure in coaching conversations comes when you tell people what to do. This doesn't develop people or leaders. You should focus on asking simple questions that will help create a much deeper connection with the person you're coaching. As an example, here are seven questions you could use, which we borrowed from the book *The Coaching Habit: Say Less, Ask More & Change the Way You Lead Forever*, by Michael Bungay Stanier:

1. What's on your mind?
2. And what else?
3. What's the real challenge here for you?
4. What do you want?
5. How can I help?
6. If you're saying yes to this, what are you saying no to?
7. What was most useful for you in this meeting?

This allows the person being coached to drive more of the conversation—where they're at, what's challenging them, places they feel they're winning, and any questions they may have—and contribute more of their ideas.

Using these questions as a guide, your discussions become more of a two-way street and focus more on the employee rather than tactics and processes. There's significantly more value in this kind of exchange for both the coach and the person being developed. You don't have to ask exactly these questions, of course. Feel free to tweak them to reflect your company and your culture. But I recommend every leader/coach use the *same* set of questions. As we discussed in the last chapter, you need a structure and process for coaching that's consistent if you want it to be successful.

One last thing to remember about these conversations: While it's our job as leaders to stretch our people and develop them, we also have to set goals that are achievable and build our employees up. Unachievable goals break people and kill the culture. Make sure your expectations match the employee, and that they're not too easy or too hard.

The most successful organizations are the ones focusing on developing their people. It's easy to say you're committed to that but much harder to actually focus the time, budget, and energy on coaching your teams. I challenge you to not only commit to coaching up front in the interview process but also periodically go back to your existing teams to reset the expectations, intentions, and desired outcomes to ensure they continue to deliver your program effectively and consistently.

WHO TO DEVELOP

In his book *Good to Great*, Jim Collins wrote, "It is better to first get the right people on the bus, the wrong people off the bus, and the right people in the right seats, and then figure out where to drive." Identifying who to best expend your development time and money on is an essential factor in rolling out your company coaching strategy. To choose effectively, you need to first understand what type of person you're dealing with and what role they play in your organization.

Amy Scott has an excellent categorization of this in her book, *Radical Candor*, one of my favorite books from the past five years. She writes that the good people on your team are either rock stars or superstars. Let me unpack the concept a little bit more.

Rock stars are those people who are currently in a management position in your company or a leadership position, and they're performing great. They've been with you for multiple years or longer. They believe in your values and are part of your brand. They show up, day in and day out. And they *love* what they do.

The mistake a lot of operators make is they try to promote rock stars. It's understandable why you would want to, but it isn't a wise decision. What you're doing is trying to promote someone

ROCK STAR vs. SUPERSTAR

The "rock star vs. superstar" concept comes from *Radical Candor* by Kim Scott

ROCK STAR

Employees who are currently in management or leadership positions and are performing great in those roles

	WHO	WHY	ACTION TO BE TAKEN
1.			
2.			
3.			
4.			
5.			

SUPERSTAR

Employees who are advancing quickly through your organization and have made it clear that they want to move up in the business

	WHO	WHY	ACTION TO BE TAKEN
1.			
2.			
3.			
4.			
5.			

mattrolfe.com

MATT ROLFE

WESTSHORE
O N L I N E

into the next role when they're happy where they are. If you're looking to scale your business—which, if you're reading this book, you are—then you're going to need people who aren't necessarily looking to grow upward but are happy to stay in their positions to *preserve* your current operating restaurants. Rock stars will be responsible for *preserving* your core. And by doing that, they'll make sure that what you build today continues to operate at an excellent level as you grow.

The people you *want* to promote are your superstars. Superstars are people who are advancing quickly through your organization. They're someone who's arrived to the team, made an impact, and made it clear they want to move up through the business. In all likelihood, if you're a senior leader and you're having a coffee or beer with this person, they're going to ask you at one point how they get your job. Superstars are those shining lights that really help you grow and expand your organization. If you try and hold a superstar back and don't give them opportunities to scale, they're going to leave your company. Growth is part of their core personality, and they will go somewhere else that lets them express those talents.

There are two things to remember when you consider your managers and leaders in terms of superstars and rock stars. The first is that you should be looking for a balance of these two types in your employees. You can't have an organization full of only rock stars or full of only superstars; it doesn't work.

The second thing to remember is that a person is not permanently a rock star or permanently a superstar. Situations change. Perhaps your manager had a baby and so they were content to stay in their role, do a good job, and focus their extra energies on their family. At that point in time, they were a rock star. But now

LEADER DEVELOPMENT PLAN

WHERE DO YOU FEEL THE LEADER IS CURRENTLY AT?	ROCK STAR OR SUPERSTAR?	PERFORMANCE	WHAT'S DRIVING THEIR CURRENT RESULT?	WHAT SUPPORT IS REQUIRED?

mattrolfe.com

the baby is older, things have quieted down, and they're ready to step into that superstar role. Or perhaps you had a superstar who advanced rapidly through the company, but now they've reached a position they like and they're more comfortable stepping back.

Essentially, be prepared to reevaluate your categorizations for your team. I encourage you to do an inventory each quarter of your people and leaders in your depth chart. Here are some questions to think about during this inventory:

- Where do you feel the person is at currently?
- Are they a rock star, or are they a superstar?
- How are they performing?
- What's the driving reason for where they are?
- How do you support them to either get to the next stage or continue to be successful in their current role?

Another exercise that's helpful when thinking about how to best develop the people in your team is Lift, Leave, Surrender. I got this from my old coach, Colin Collard. When you're reflecting on your people, think about who in your company is in a position to *lift* the business up. More often than not, these will be your superstars, and they're the ones you should be looking to promote and grow with you.

Then think about, in Jack Welch's terminology, the bottom 20 percent of your people who have consistently stayed in that position. These are people who don't seem to be moving up the organization or are underperforming in their roles. Let them leave or help them leave; they'll move on to opportunities better suited to them. (I'm not saying go and fire them immediately after your

LIFT, LEAVE, SURRENDER

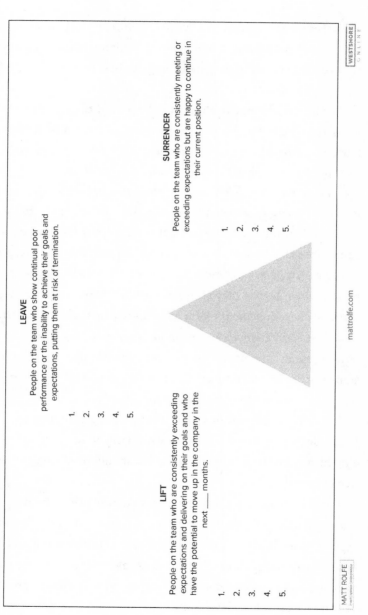

LEAVE

People on the team who show continual poor performance or the inability to achieve their goals and expectations, putting them at risk of termination.

1.

2.

3.

4.

5.

SURRENDER

People on the team who are consistently meeting or exceeding expectations but are happy to continue in their current position.

1.

2.

3.

4.

5.

LIFT

People on the team who are consistently exceeding expectations and delivering on their goals and who have the potential to move up in the company in the next ____ months.

1.

2.

3.

4.

5.

MATT ROLFE

WESTSHORE ONLINE

mattrolfe.com

analysis and assessment. As I've said before, give them an opportunity to improve. But if they no longer align with your values or they're consistently underperforming, it's best to let them go—for both of your sakes.)

And lastly, we come to the *Surrender* part of the exercise. Many of us have been taught that "surrender" is a word of weakness, but Colin showed me that "surrender" is a term of power. Look at your people and ask yourself, *who am I going to surrender to?* There are people who we poke, we jab, and we *push*, when the reality is they're doing great where they are. They're not ready to move. They don't want to. Sometimes these are your rock stars, and sometimes they're people who just need a bit more time to grow at their own pace. Surrender to the fact that they're going to be great in the role that they're in and nothing more. They're going to work on these specific projects and expose themselves to nothing new. Just allow them to be great and develop. It's not always about advancement. Sometimes people just need to breathe in the positions they're in. Once we see "surrender" as a word of power and not weakness, this becomes easier for us to do.

If you're rapidly scaling your team, I suggest doing the Lift, Leave, Surrender exercise on a monthly basis. It helps identify who should stay on the bus and where they should be seated and who needs to get off.

Identifying potential leaders isn't something that just happens once and then you can forget about it. You need to do this on a regular basis. If every rock-star employee gets promoted and you don't have a foundation of others in development, it creates structural instability in your business. Be sure to focus time on growing your bench as well as developing your current top performers.

TAKING IT SLOW

High performers always want to know what they need to do to get the next job. In coaching their development, you need to reframe this expectation: the next job requires more than just raw talent—it requires top performance in the existing position. They need to be great where they are and have a little bit of patience as well. Just being a great young leader doesn't entitle them to the next opportunity.

When I was twenty-three years old, I walked into the office of my boss, Brent Quartermain, and asked him to be my mentor. This was a gutsy move for a kid, considering Brent was the big boss and had a dominant persona that scared me a bit. Lucky for me, Brent agreed, taking the time to work with me during and after my employment at Labatt. Brent always said that the first year in a role, you learn the ropes; the second year, you should dominate; and in year three, "we find out who you are." I'm not saying everyone should be in a role for three years, but they should be given an appropriate amount of time to settle, get the benefit of being a new leader, and show whether they can consistently perform.

I caution against pushing people forward too quickly, even your superstars. One of the biggest reasons people leave the industry is they get promoted to a position they aren't ready for yet. Overexposing someone by putting them in an overly difficult situation like that leads to burnout and unnecessary employee turnover.

I have experienced this firsthand. One of our employees was hired at an hourly rate and quickly showed himself to be a leader. We were growing so fast during the first three or five years that we kept putting him in positions without the proper training and support. Eventually, he came to me and said he needed to take a year off because he was so burnt out. It was one of the most heartbreaking conversations I've ever had—we'd basically built the company around him.

When he returned, I offered him the General Manager position. Essentially, I was asking him to run the entire company. He said no. Based on his previous experience, he didn't feel he was ready. Although I was disappointed in this decision then, I now see what a mistake it would have been if he'd accepted the job at that stage of his career. Today, after getting more experience, development, and years under his belt, he is our CEO.

Think of this as a cautionary tale when you're itching to promote someone based on a need rather than their readiness. You need to protect your leaders from being moved through the system too quickly. A true top performer is used to winning. If you put them in a position where they never win, they will quit. Instead, temper their growth, for your benefit and theirs. And don't count out your hourly employees when deciding who is worthy of your development investment!

If you develop a good coaching strategy and train your leaders on how to effectively coach, you'll create an unstoppable team.

From the last few chapters, you now know how crucial it is to communicate candidly with your team, invest in your people's development, and execute (learned) coaching that's beneficial for your people's growth. These aspects are essential to building out a tribe that can support your organization as you scale and push your company in the direction you want to go so that you're playing to win.

But to execute those high-level concepts to see *results*, you need meetings.

Consistent meetings.

KEY TAKEAWAYS

- Not everyone knows how to coach—it's a learned skill! If you want an effective coaching strategy throughout your organization, you'll have to teach them.

- When creating a coaching strategy, lift from where you stand.

- Always create a schedule for coaching so that it can be implemented consistently throughout your organization.

- What you coach will depend on your company and where you want to go.

- Structure your coaching conversations so that it's (a) consistent throughout the organization and (b) your leaders are trained to allow the person being developed to drive the conversation and discuss what matters to them.

- Your people are either rock stars or superstars. Each needs to be treated differently.

- The Lift, Leave, Surrender exercise helps you choose who to develop in your organization

- Don't push people forward too quickly—even your superstars.

CHAPTER 9

COMMUNICATION AND MEETING RHYTHM

"A leader's first priority is to create an
environment where others can do things, and
that cannot happen if they are not effective."
—Patrick Lencioni

'll be honest with you: the difference between average-performing groups and high-performing groups is meetings. I've seen it in the dozens and dozens of teams I coach, especially restaurant teams. Top-performing groups have a structured and planned meeting rhythm that sets the cadence for communication across the team.

We can't do it, Matt. I can see you throw up your hands, shake your head. *We're too busy—we work in operations! We can't possibly spend more time in meetings.*

But you must, if you want to be the top-performing group you set out to be when you began this book. So, let's examine your resistance. Why do you think you can't make more time for meetings? There's probably a very simple answer for it: you're not seeing enough value in the meetings you already hold.

Take a moment to think about how meetings are run in your company. Think about their structure, length, and frequency. Most restaurant groups think they're holding one meeting a week, which is probably this catch-all management meeting, and an annual conference where you bring the team together. That's the time they've set aside. But the reality is, you're having more meetings than that. These meetings are happening in hallways, in one-on-one conversations, in water-cooler chats, but they are happening. Look at your time audit (we covered this in Chapter 6), and you'll see it. And those "meetings" are not as useful for your company. They don't end in decision, alignment, or execution-focused strategy. They get the job done, sure, but you could be doing it better.

The foundations of a meeting are clear intentions and outcome and passionate and positive conflict. Every meeting you go into should have a clearly framed intention and outcome. "Passionate, positive conflict" does not mean fighting, but it does mean that once the team is clear on its goals, you should have the conversations that need to be had.

That's what this chapter is about. How do you structure meetings in your organization so that all conversation is directed toward your goals? I get the resistance to meetings—I do. But as Tony Robbins said, "If you want to produce great results, model someone who's already doing it." The top-performing restaurant groups in North America are doing it. If you're a restaurant group looking to grow, then it's time to implement a meeting rhythm that meets the needs of your organization.

QUARTERLY OFFSITES

Senior leaders should get together at least once a quarter to review progress and discuss what needs to be done to reach your goals for the year.

Quarterly meetings should allow departments to present where they stand versus their goals, without allowing silos to form. You don't want marketing to say they're winning while operations is letting everyone down. This is the time for everyone to come together, see what's working and what isn't, and brainstorm how to improve.

These meetings ideally should last two days and be held off-site. I'm a big believer in putting your people in a position of full immersion. If you hold your meeting in an office boardroom and four o'clock comes around, then everyone is checking their watches. They're thinking about picking up their kids, going back to their emails, and answering that operator who has been demanding their attention all day. When four o'clock strikes, they aren't fully present.

A two-day, off-site changes that. It creates a captured environment where they've got nowhere to run, and they know that months before heading into it. It allows space for connection. You're not just in meetings. You're having dinner together. You're doing an activity, like a hike or a game of golf, where you get into your body and get moving. These downtimes matter. They create context, trust, and momentum as well as give the team some space to *ease* into the meetings.

QUARTERLY MEETING AGENDA I DAY 1

LIGHTNING ROUND ONE-WORD OPEN

SCOREBOARD
Core focus/How we win

LEADER UPDATES
Ahead of Plan

On Plan

Off Plan

TEAM COMMUNICATION
What's working?

Core focus/Critical drivers

Key metrics/Core projects

What's not?

STRATEGIC DISCUSSION
Problems to solve

DISCUSSION, ACTION, COMMITMENT REVIEW
Discussion

Action

Alignment discussion

Commitment

CASCADING COMMUNICATION
What

Who

How

Why

MATT ROLFE

mattrolfe.com

WESTSHORE
ONLINE

QUARTERLY MEETING AGENDA | DAY 2

WHAT ARE WE GOING TO DO?	WHY ARE WE DOING IT?	WHO IS RESPONSIBLE/ACCOUNTABLE?	WHEN ARE WE GOING TO DO IT?
1.			
2.			
3.			
4.			
5.			

MATT ROLFE

mattrolfe.com

WESTSHORE ONLINE

During these quarterly offsites, I like to use team-building exercises to further connect people and build relationships. One of my favorites is having everyone take a personality profile inventory. This helps everyone understand how to best communicate with each other—a skill leaders can utilize in developing their own teams once the offsite is over. Learning about communication styles helps ensure everyone is on the same page.

Day one should focus on where you've been as a company—your operation's results so far. Day two should focus on how to get where you want to go—how your operation will achieve your goals going forward. The meeting then wraps with very clear communication about how, when, and by whom the information discussed there will get disseminated to others inside the company. This is the concept of cascading communications that we talked about in Chapter 6, "Candid Communication." It's very important to decide what you're going to share, as well as how, why, and by when, so there are no assumptions or miscommunications.

Structuring your offsite over two days rather than one day gives you the time to execute this schedule properly. Two of the most crucial elements to get right here are the introduction to your quarterly offsite, where you create engagement among your team, and your closing, where you cover cascading communication. To do these well, you need two hours to half a day for each. Squeezing them into a shorter timeframe or rushing them will impact how your team engages with the offsite and what messages they take away.

I can promise that if you set aside eight days a year to do these quarterly offsites, you'll see the benefits not only in results but also in the culture and connection in your team.

MONTHLY STRATEGY MEETINGS

Once a month, plan an off-site, half- to full-day meeting with senior leaders down through location management. The morning should focus on updates from the senior leader as well as allow each department to present where they are tracking in terms of goals. The afternoon should be set aside for coming together as a group to solve an interesting or unique problem or opportunity your business is facing. The goal is to brainstorm ideas that will have the biggest impact on your results by working together as a team. It also creates the opportunity for passionate, positive conflict and improves engagement so everyone is aligned. This meeting ends with clarity on who is responsible for what and how to communicate that.

There is a formula to a successful monthly meeting. First, leaders have a template or one-pager, created prior to the meeting, which is linked to their goals or their department's goals. They fill it out to show progress. Second, there is consistent structure about what's shared.

Start the meeting with a clear update of where your team is versus the core goals—a fact-based update on your team's performance for the last month as it relates to your goals. Next comes a positive opening we call a "one-word open." Each person says how they are feeling in a single word. This provides a feel for the room. If someone shares something indicating they're stuck or not engaged, stop, isolate that, and take the time to get everyone involved and fully participating.

Then move into positive openings: a tactical way to shift the state of the room by having everyone reflect on one positive win—

MONTHLY MEETING AGENDA

LIGHTNING ROUND ONE-WORD OPEN

LEADER UPDATES
Ahead of Plan

On Plan

Off Plan

SCOREBOARD
Core focus/How we win

Core focus/Critical drivers

Key metrics/Core projects

TEAM COMMUNICATION
What's working?

What's not?

CASCADING COMMUNICATION
What

Who

How

Why

DISCUSSION, ACTION, COMMITMENT REVIEW
Discussion

Action

Commitment

PEOPLE PERFORMANCE REVIEW
Lift

Leave

Surrender

MATT ROLFE

mattrolfe.com

WESTSHORE
ONLINE

for themself, their teams, or their goals—from the previous month. You want them to see there are positive patterns for themselves and their teams. Individuals get sixty seconds each.

Too often, we go too deep on content too soon in a meeting. This process allows you to lean into the meeting by acclimatizing to the space a little bit.

FEELING CHART

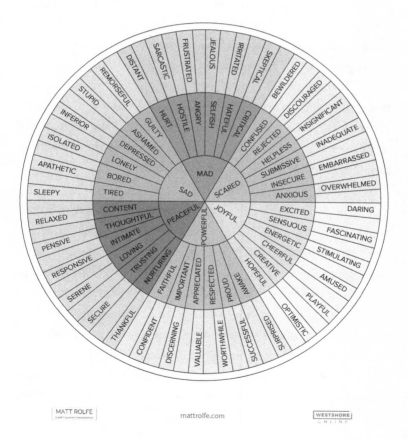

WEEKLY MEETINGS

Here's what I find is the biggest break of trust around meetings. Most teams that I coach have weekly meetings that are scheduled to run between ninety minutes and two hours. When I ask them what's on the agenda, the answer is always generic, *Whatever we need to discuss in the week.*

When I start to peel the onion back a little bit—and it is like an onion, because it makes people cry—I find out that what they're doing in these meetings is discussing *everything.* Every single discussion, whether it's relevant to the group or only one leader in the room, gets crammed into that meeting slot. And it grows, bloats, and spills over. What is supposed to be a ninety-minute to two-hour meeting runs over three hours. Dave is missing his kid's soccer practice, so he's disengaged and pissed off. Sally is frustrated simply coming into the room because she knows these meetings have no structure and focus. No one's happy.

This is why people hate meetings.

Turtle Jack's suffered from this problem. I loved the team running Muskoka Grill; they were fantastic people, and they *loved* each other. They all got along like a house on fire. But each week, when they entered the room to have their weekly meetings, something would shift. I saw it firsthand. The energy would drop. People's body language would change. And that was because these meetings wouldn't *end.* They'd be scheduled for ninety minutes to two hours, and then they'd go on for *half a day.* Sometimes more. There were times that team was still sitting in the conference room as the sky went dark, the lights came on, and they'd missed dinner.

WEEKLY MEETING AGENDA

LIGHTNING ROUND ONE-WORD OPEN

SCOREBOARD

Core focus/How we win

Core focus/Critical drivers

Key metrics/Core projects

LEADER UPDATES

On Plan

Off Plan

Need Help

Impact on Other Departments

STRATEGIC DISCUSSION

Problems to solve

Alignment discussion

DISCUSSION, ACTION, COMMITMENT REVIEW

Discussion

Action

Commitment

CASCADING COMMUNICATION

What

Who

How

Why

MATT ROLFE

mattrolfe.com

WESTSHORE
ONLINE

The problem was exactly what you think it is: they were trying to tackle too much in one conversation. It wasn't possible to deal with all the topics they needed in an in-depth manner in *one* meeting. If you're also having weekly meetings that feel like they go on forever and don't get much accomplished, then you're suffering from the same problem.

The first thing I did with Turtle Jack's was to get them to acknowledge that there was a problem—this structure wasn't working for anyone. Then we started to talk about what these weekly meetings were really for. What was the intention? Once we knew that, we could shape an agenda and keep the meeting on track.

I want you to do the same thing. You do need weekly meetings, but you need to make sure you have a clear intention for them and you choose that intention wisely. Ask yourself, *Why are we bringing this group of people together inside our company at this frequency?* When you have clear answers, your meeting will have a clear intention and outcome; it won't meander. And, like Turtle Jack's, you'll begin to see results. By simply clarifying their intentions and outcomes, Turtle Jack's meetings went from more than four hours to running within ninety minutes to two hours.

That's great, you're thinking, *but we still need to discuss everything that needs to be discussed that week.*

I agree, which is why I encourage you to splinter off and create other meetings as needed to take the pressure off your weekly meeting. I call these "weekly project meetings," but essentially they're consistent and reoccurring meetings focused around company projects, company initiatives, or certain teams. Once you've identified your intention and outcomes for your main weekly meeting, distribute the appropriate people, topics, intentions, and outcomes that are still left to these other meetings. Each of them will only include the relevant leaders, so you won't be pulling everyone into a room to listen to things that don't concern them.

DAILY TOUCH POINTS

I'm a huge fan of *Mastering the Rockefeller Habits* by Verne Harnish. The first month we started our company, my two business partners and I would go through it every Tuesday at the Greasy Spoon in Schomburg, Ontario. The number one thing we took from that book and have made part of our companies from that point on is the daily touchpoint.

Daily touchpoints consist of a five- to fifteen-minute check-in every morning where everyone shares whether they're on track to meet their goals in a red, yellow, green format. Green means you're on track, yellow means you're close but need to catch up in a couple of areas, and red means you're off track. When people share they're off track, it allows us to find out what additional support they need. It's also a chance for people to ask any critical questions that need to be shared to make sure we can keep moving forward in the direction of our goals.

I highly recommend instituting a daily touchpoint in your organization—it does wonders to connect the team and infuse the day with the right energy. They don't take a lot of time at all: the daily touchpoints in my company take place at 3:30 p.m. and they last for eight minutes maximum. Doing the same kind of group huddle inside your restaurants every day can ensure your team is focused on what matters most, determine if there's anything getting in the way, and allow people to ask for help if necessary.

MANAGING MEETINGS EFFECTIVELY

I first heard Cameron Herold speak at the Global Leadership Conference organized by the Entrepreneurs' Organization. There were all these great speakers, and then suddenly, there's this guy walking toward a room and he's been mobbed. Literally mobbed, like he's a rock star. I didn't know what was going on. His room was packed, standing room only. And there were all these people hovering near him, trying to get a piece of his time. I was so intrigued, I stayed to listen.

Cameron gave a fantastic keynote speech at that conference. One of the things he talked about was a concept in his book *Double Double* that then became the groundwork for his next book, *Meetings Suck*. If you haven't read *Meetings Suck*, I highly recommend it. What he said in the book and in that keynote speech was, "No agenda, no attendance."

If the meeting has no agenda, then Cameron wasn't going to attend. Nor was his team. It's a concept you see a lot of great leaders adopt. Tony Robbins, for instance, asks at the beginning of every conversation or meeting, "What's the intention and outcome that we desire from this meeting?" And if he can't get that clear, he literally keeps walking. He doesn't have time to stick around. But if you *have* that agenda, if you have that intention and outcome clear, then the focus of your time can be incredible. I've seen Tony Robbins hold concentrated fifteen-minute meetings backstage while 3,000 people were doing his workshop out front.

I've taken Cameron's words of "no agenda, no attendance" deeply to heart. If there isn't an agenda, there's no reason for any team to be brought together and invest company time in a room.

My team follows this. We have timeframes for each meeting, and we draw up an agenda either twenty-four hours or forty-eight hours in advance, depending on the type of meeting. If there's no agenda, I walk out of the room. I've taken it so much to heart, I tell my clients the same thing.

I have a client that brings the exact same twelve people into a room once a week for three hours, and there's absolutely no intention to that meeting. They're spending over $300,000 of overhead and time in that room on an annual basis. But they won't make an agenda. So I stopped going. I told them, *I love you guys, and I'm happy to keep working with you, but that meeting—no. Not happening.*

People do get extremely upset about it. One client was furious when I told them twenty-four hours before a workshop that I wasn't coming because it wasn't focused on an agenda. I wasn't doing it to be a dick. I was doing it to prove what the benefit of an agenda could be to a conversation. All of us love to talk. We just don't like to commit to action, deadlines, and execution. This book is about the difference between average and top performing—and that's one of the keys. I'm happy to have a client furious at me if it means they have an agenda for the rest of their meetings. It means I did my job.

So the first thing to do for all of your meetings—*get an agenda.*

Also be sure to include a component of accountability in every meeting: who will do what by when? Make a commitment to doing the things you're discussing, and follow up to ensure they get done. Focusing on three core drivers rather than having ten random goals helps keep your team from overcommitting and under-delivering as a result.

Honing down the list of things you are holding people accountable for lets them complete tasks with excellence rather than trying to do a lot of things with mediocre results. There's no worse culture killer than allowing people to get overcommitted and then feel like failures when they cannot complete their assigned tasks.

Decide beforehand how you'll handle off-topic questions or comments that are better addressed "offline"—meaning outside of the meeting and probably among a much smaller subset of the people attending. Some leaders use a hand motion to signal this while others jot down a note on a whiteboard. The purpose of this is to keep the meeting moving along while at the same time remembering to circle back to the offline topic at a later moment. This ensures your agenda doesn't get overloaded and your meeting doesn't run over time-wise.

The bottom line is you want your meeting to deliver the right experience, connection, or conversation. In the restaurant industry, our communication often comes as a result of an urgent reaction to a guest or staff member, which isn't always helpful. Organized and well-planned meetings should help people experience proactive and positive communication, not reactive and negative communication.

If you create a meeting rhythm for your company and follow it consistently, then I promise you that you'll be able to direct your people's energies toward the strategies we've discussed in the previous chapters, and you'll see results in your company's scale and bottom line.

We are almost at the end of the book now—you're only one chapter away from your execution-focused strategy that will help you implement the ideas in the book. But before we get there, I want to linger one more time on you.

We opened this book with you: with the burden on your shoulders and the panic you felt at being at capacity. I told you then you couldn't do it alone, and then I showed in these pages just how you could do it. I hope there have been "aha!" moments as you read this and that you've seen a path toward change in these pages.

But now it's time to tackle your investment in yourself. Your organization won't grow if you don't take the time to develop yourself as a person, not just as a leader. Because, as we all know, consciousness starts at the top, as does leadership development and growth.

✕

KEY TAKEAWAYS

- A consistent meeting rhythm is what separates top performers from average performers.

- You probably hate meetings because you're not seeing any value in them right now. You can change that by defining an ideal intention and outcome for your meetings.

- An ideal meeting rhythm is:
  - Quarterly offsites
  - Monthly strategy meetings
  - Weekly meetings (and weekly project meetings)
  - Daily touch points

- All meetings need to have an agenda. Remember Cameron Herold's words: "No agenda, no attendance."

- Create a strategy for how to handle accountability in your meetings.

CHAPTER 10

INVEST IN YOURSELF

"The best investment you can make is in yourself."
—Warren Buffet

I t was Kit Andrews who taught me the importance of personal development. You've met him before in these pages—he was one of my customers when I was working for Labatt Breweries, now owned by Anheuser-Busch, then he became my first business partner, and now he's one of my best friends. He changed what I believed possible.

Kit was one of the first people to look at my career, look at me, and say, *Matt, I believe in you. I believe you can do great things.*

No one had said that to me before. To hear that, after the school experience I'd had, after teachers told me I wouldn't graduate high school—it touched me deeply. But Kit wasn't done. *I am going to help you harness that ability*, he said. *All that greatness is possible—as long as you invest in your personal development.*

And I knew what he meant. Kit's one of the smartest people I've met, but he didn't even graduate high school. It wasn't his school that made him brilliant and smart. It was his investment in himself.

How do I start? I asked, leaning forward.

What's the last book you read? he said.

I was twenty-five years old then. I honestly don't think I'd completed a book. I *may* have listened to an audiobook on sales. I told Kit the honest answer: *none.*

Let me be clear, he said. *That's not an option moving forward.*

That's how my journey into personal development began. We'd just started our business and Kit bought me a car—I didn't have one of my own because I'd just handed over the keys to the company vehicle to my old place of work. The car he bought was a Ford Probe, which was dated by about ten years even at that point. Luckily enough, it did have a tape player. We turned the car into a library. I was driving four to five hours at a time, going to new markets because we were expanding the franchises. I'd pop a tape in, listen to an audiobook, and get through a book a week. Every Tuesday, we'd meet for breakfast at Greasy Spoon in Schomburg, Ontario, and review the chapters of the books we'd committed to reading. Those breakfasts were wonderful; they were a way to slow down and connect as we launched a business. I learned later that Kit had already read a lot of those books, but he read them again with me. It made all the difference. He wasn't telling me to go read a book. He was actually helping me create a habit as he read the exact same book and followed the exact same process at the same time.

Kit taught me how to invest in myself. I learned how to grapple with the insecurity of how small teachers made me feel in high school, of being told I was stupid and a failure. Personal development is now a deep passion for me. For the last decade, I've always ensured I have a personal coach, someone who develops me as a leader. I've been involved in peer groups. Kit sponsored me to join the Entrepreneurs' Organization, which is the most impactful organization I've ever joined in my life. It surrounds me with like-minded people and exposes me to incredible experiences. I also invest in Masterminds, including Brad Hart's Make More Marbles. We believe Brad is the best coach in this space. He coaches leaders on creating and executing Masterminds, and he has his own, which puts us in the community of like-minded leaders focused on bringing group learning to their niche. As we write this, I'm part of the KBB Accelerator Program for coaches. I attend conferences. And I always read: I go through a long list of audiobooks each year to continue to develop myself.

I invest more in my personal development than I do in stocks, in my retirement savings plans, or in my business because it's proven to have the best ROI. And we invest in the same personal development strategies for *every* leader on our team.

All this is to say I know the value that personal development can bring to leadership and to your organization. Often, leadership isn't only about business tactics and leadership methods—it's about you as a person. You began reading this book because you want to scale your company to the next level; I'm here to tell you that you can't do it without also scaling yourself.

In this chapter, I'll talk you through some of the tactics, methods, and devices you can use to invest in your personal development.

WHY ROUTINE MATTERS

One thing every successful entrepreneur, leader, athlete, and musician has in common is specific patterns—routines and behaviors they followed religiously to help them succeed in their respective field. Warren Buffet, Mark Cuban, and Michael Jordan each committed countless hours to these patterns to achieve their superstar standing. Building strong routines like they did is key to your personal development: it helps you achieve your goals, both at work and in your personal life.

It's not just positive patterns you have to pay attention to. You also need to look out for habits that are negatively affecting you as a person. One simple practice I see my clients do that severely impacts the rest of their day is this: they wake up and reach for their phone. They look at their social media feeds; they check their email. This means they're bombarded with other people's interests, challenges, and problems. Studies show this can actually damage your productivity (not to mention your mood). The biggest concern here is you're immediately taking on other people's urgency or problems rather than focusing on your success. You're programming fear and negative feelings into your body first thing in the morning and training yourself to think when you open your eyes, *What's wrong now?*

Don't touch your phone in the morning. In fact, work on tackling your general addiction to technology. All of these apps and systems are designed to keep us dependent on our screens; work on shaking off that habit.

Another negative pattern that emerges over time is *I was all work and no play*. I actually hear this one a lot in Entrepreneurs'

Organization. These are incredible people who've built businesses up from nothing. I look at most of them and think, *Wow, they're so successful*. But what emerges in our forum meetings is this refrain of *I wish I did it differently*. All these highly respected business leaders are sitting there and saying *I didn't invest time in my personal life. I didn't spend time with my family. I ignored my health*. They had great businesses, but their wives had left them. They were at risk of a heart attack. Their kids weren't answering their phone calls. And it wasn't worth it.

Don't make the same mistake. Invest in aspects of your life other than business. Give your time to the people you love. And make time for self-care.

Self-care is a squishy word with many definitions, so let me clarify what I mean by it. Are you finding a way to make an investment in yourself each day? Basketball legend Kobe Bryant always said he was trying to be one percent better today than he was yesterday. What are you doing to get slightly better every day? Make an investment in improvement. Are you making time to do something that fuels you? We'll go into establishing a daily routine in the next section, so you'll see what my definition of self-care looks like there. But it could be really simple: Listening to twenty minutes of an audiobook. Exercising. Writing in a gratitude journal. Just make sure you're creating a period of time each day where you take your foot off the gas pedal, breathe, and invest in yourself.

And it has to be frequent. A vacation isn't self-care. It's *good* for you and you may need it, but it's not self-care. Nor is the massage you take once in six months. If the only time I invest in myself is one hour every six months, I'm in big trouble. You need to find a way to decompress each day.

I can tell you that there have been times in my life when I haven't invested in self-care, and it has had a ripple effect. It showed up as overeating, overdrinking, and substance abuse. That's in my past now. But those are the risks you run when you don't take care of yourself. And the health risks it creates, especially as you get older, are astronomical.

I get it—self-care is difficult to do. You already have a full plate; how are you going to make time for this? I used to struggle too. I've had two therapists in my life who've never met each other and they both asked me what I do for myself in the day. When I answered them, they laughed. (I don't think therapists are supposed to laugh.) They both said, *I don't believe you.* And they were right; I wasn't really doing it. But I do it now, and I've seen the difference it makes.

As a coach, I help my clients identify the patterns and habits that are helping them reach their goals and the ones that are hindering their achievement. I start by asking, *Think of three times you've achieved a goal, and then identify what you did to allow that result to happen.* You don't need more than three answers (remember the Rule of Three) to find a pattern. The answer might be in the speed at which you did the task, the team you assembled to reach the goal, or how consistent you were about practicing that particular skill daily.

Next I ask, *Now think of three times you didn't get the buy-in or result you expected, and why you didn't achieve what you wanted.* Perhaps the answer is that the action required to meet the goal and the clarity of who was accountable for each step was missing or that you weren't able to spend enough time on it because you were overcommitted elsewhere.

ESTABLISHING A HEALTHY ROUTINE

Establishing a healthy daily routine that practices all of the positive habits you want to keep and weeds out the negative ones is key to creating more energy, more focus, and better fulfillment.

My morning routine has served me well personally and professionally. It allows me to show up at work with the right energy and mindset, and make time for self-care. I wake up every day at 5:00 a.m. and drink a glass of lemon water. I do this no matter where I am in the world, even when I'm traveling a lot. It's just that part of the routine that makes me feel grounded and consistent.

I then read ten pages of a book I'm working through and write a bit in my gratitude journal. That's my version of self-care; something that fuels *me*. A workout is next. I'm also working on five to ten minutes of guided meditation. Anyone who knows me knows my mind vibrates at a pretty quick pace; I don't know if I'll ever be a master at meditation, but I spend those minutes trying to silence my mind and be present in my body.

Then I'm up and choosing what clothes to wear for the day. I create simple choices for myself here. I have a standard outfit. A lot of leaders do this: Barack Obama, Mark Zuckerberg, and Arianna Huffington, to name a few. I follow their lead. I'm not spending a lot of time and energy in the morning wondering what I'm going to wear.

By then, it's 8:00 a.m. I'll spend from 8:00 a.m. to 9:00 a.m. on the most critical project we have going on in our business; I give it my undivided attention. From 9:00 a.m. onward, I open my door to other people. I get on a 9:00 a.m. call with my business partner where we focus on critical decision-making: What is the focus for our business? What needs to be decided? Where are we going and are we on track? And then I get into calls and emails—I put myself at the service of others.

Carving out that time between 5:00 a.m. to 8:00 a.m. for myself has been critical for how much energy and focus I can bring to the rest of the day. It was reinforced two years ago by Jack Canfield, who is one of the best development coaches on the planet. He talked about how he had to reset himself thanks to all the technological distractions in our world, and he now spends three hours focused on the most important priority for himself.

A night routine is as important as a morning routine. My daughter really shaped my night routines. When she was three years old, she said to me, *Daddy, when we're together at night, you're there, but you're always working on your phone.*

That hit home. My father was an entrepreneur. He did an incredible job of providing for us, but he was always working. And he missed my childhood. Hearing my daughter say that made it clear to me that I could miss hers. I was physically there each night, but I wasn't present. As she said, *You need to play with me.*

So that's what I do now. My phone is off, and I mark out this time to be with family. I play with my daughter—it grounds me—and have dinner with my wife. I stay present. Then at about 8:30 p.m., I do a little bit of closeout at work. Then I shut off.

Committing to a personal routine makes it much easier to commit to a work routine. Start by listing the things you need to do on a daily basis. Focus on what matters most for your businesses, teams, and your own results. Establishing a work routine ensures you're investing your time in what's important for you and your team's success rather than just being reactive and paying attention to someone else's urgency.

Plan when and for how long you'll touch base with your team and check email. Remember the eight-to-thirteen rule, and block the time to attend to your routine on your calendar. There are no right or wrong times to complete your daily activities. The important thing is to be as consistent as possible.

It's also important to realize that after a certain point, there is a diminishing return on the hours you put into work. There's a reason I shut down around 10:00 p.m. We all have the ability to work till midnight or later, but is it actually getting the results you want? For instance, if you're not obviously seeing the benefit of working more than sixty hours, acknowledge that as your limit. Surrender to your optimal hours. The mountain of work is never going to go away, so you need to ask yourself, *How can I be in the right state or energy to produce the best result?*

Of course you won't be able to account for every hour or even minute of your day. But having a routine helps put you in the right energy and state of mind to produce the results. Questions to see if your current routine is helping you move forward include:

- Is my routine working for me?
- What can I change to improve, get better results, or be in a better frame of mind each day?
- What results are my habits creating for my people?

AVOIDING OVERCOMMITMENT

If you're a leader and an operator, then you're used to pushing yourself. You're used to being at capacity and still reaching to find ways to get things done.

Rein yourself in. Remember, there's always another mountain to climb. Your work is never going to be done. There is no finish line.

It's much more important to ask yourself: Is my routine sustainable? Will it allow me to take the business to the next level? (If you're overcommitting, the answer is no.)

Overcommitment does not improve your productivity. In fact, it is entirely detrimental. In addition, your relationships—with your employees, family, friends, and yourself—suffer greatly because of it as well. Your team will feel they need to work as many hours as you do or they'll end up disappointed in themselves and their ability to perform. If you see your people sending emails at midnight because that's what you do, it's time to make a change. No one wants to lose connection with their friends or feel they have no identity outside of the business. Tell yourself taking time to have a personal life matters, and so does participating in activities you love with the people you love.

WORKING WITH A COACH

All top-performing athletes, entrepreneurs, and leaders have coaches. You'll find that the larger the organization, the more common a coach becomes. My passion is to provide access to coaching to the hospitality entrepreneurs and leaders of our industry as well as create a peer group for the hospitality industry that doesn't currently exist.

But what does good coaching look like? I've studied who I believe are the best coaches, and I've identified a process that repeats across all the big names. You can go look up a Colin Collard or Brendon Burchard, and this model of interactions will be the same.

Here's how it works. The best model of frequency for coaching is a recurring call with your coach. I usually recommend a biweekly call that runs between ninety minutes and two hours, but this depends on the needs of the leader. You could do a weekly call, but I like biweekly more because it gives you some time to breathe, absorb, and act before the next call. These calls also give you a frequency of accountability as you revisit what you discussed on the last call.

The second key element of coaching is that two days a quarter—ideally, two consecutive days—are invested in immersion strategy sessions. These are similar to the quarterly offsites I mentioned last chapter. If someone wants to coach with us and can't commit to this, then we don't engage in coaching with them. These sessions are crucial. If you're a senior leader and your leadership team is growing rapidly, then you need this time to sit down in the same room and dive deep into where the leaders are and where they're stuck. We look at what the opportunities are and what our execution plan is. The aim is to make sure we're taking in enough data based on our recent performance and also moving *forward* toward our goals. It also helps us ensure we're intentional in the direction, projects, and efforts we're putting into the business—that the goals we're running toward are the right ones.

If you're really committed to making significant change for you and your team, then a coach isn't a "nice-to-have" at this stage. It's necessary. All large organizations know this; the bigger the organization, the more common a coach becomes. Define the budget you have to invest in yourself—and make the time commitment!—to ensure you have the support you need to develop at the pace you want and move your business in the right direction.

Investing in yourself is an essential part of leadership. So is execution. In the next chapter, I'll show how to put what I've taught you into action.

✕

KEY TAKEAWAYS

- Leadership isn't only about business tactics and leadership methods—it's about you as a person.

- I invest the most in my personal development because it's proven to have the best ROI.

- Identify positive patterns that fill you with the right energy to start your day. Distance yourself from your negative patterns.

- Disconnect from technology for part of each day.

- Don't invest too much in your work life at the cost of your personal life. Your profession is not all you are.

- Make time for consistent self-care. It could be anything—reading a book, writing in a gratitude journal, or listening to a podcast. Make sure it is frequent.

- A good morning and evening routine offers rhythm to your personal life and your work life. Establish one.

- Overcommitment does not improve your productivity.

- If you're really committed to making significant change for you and your team, then a coach isn't a "nice-to-have" at this stage. It's necessary.

CHAPTER 11

EXECUTION-FOCUSED STRATEGY

"Innovation is rewarded.
Execution is worshipped."

—Eric Thomas

I promised you in the Introduction to this book that I would give you the tools to implement everything you've learned in these pages and that I was committed to driving you from idea to action.

I meant it.

When I look back at the first five years of my coaching, I realize a lot of failures came from failing to take my clients from this idea stage to the action stage. I would go into boardrooms with 150 people. I'd lead workshops and give keynotes speeches. And by the end, everyone was fired up. These were great, transformational ideas! People were excited, and they couldn't wait to implement them. They would come up to me after the session and ask to stay connected.

It felt *great*. I felt like I was doing what I was meant to do: help people.

But then I'd run into these people on the street, at future conferences, and at lectures. I'd say, *Hey! How did that idea work out for your business?* And 90 percent of the time, people would look at me with guilt and shame in their eyes. They'd say, *Oh, we really loved that. But we got back to our business, we got busy, and we didn't do it.*

That really affected me as a coach. I was classifying these workshops and talks as "strategy creation"—but really, they were just entertainment. If the ideas didn't get to a point where they were implemented in a business, then all those concepts were just performance. It reached a point where I began asking myself: Could I keep doing this? Did I *want* to keep doing this? There's a big business for coaches to write books, speak consistently, and have no accountability to results. But when I connected with myself, I found my passion isn't just communicating ideas. My passion is shifting people *through* action to get the results they want and deserve.

The key to doing that, to making sure you don't just add this book to your endless pile of "how-tos" that you never revisit, is getting *clear* on how you take action. What are you going to do in the next 100 days to ensure the content from this book or any "aha!" moment you had going through it helps shift your business in the right direction?

The way to know that, to be clear about it, is making sure you anchor in an *execution*-focused strategy.

100-DAY EXECUTION PLAN

I first learned of the 100-day program from author, speaker, and coach Joey Coleman. Joey came to the Toronto Chapter of Entrepreneurs' Organization and gave one of the most impactful speeches I've heard. He talked about his 100-day execution plan to help companies build a strategy to keep every customer that they interacted with. He wanted to know: *How do you never lose a customer inside your business? How do you stay connected with them?*

What Joey showed us was a process for keeping in touch with a customer for the first 100 days after they interact with your company. It contained twenty-six interactions and was supported by statistics from banks and cell phone companies who use a similar process to keep your contact details and make sure they stay in touch with you.

I want you to put together a similar 100-day execution plan. I want you to outline what *exactly* needs to happen in the next 100 days to change the trajectory of your business. Here is a sample of the information you need to map out your 100-day execution plan. Complete the first few weeks as shown, but don't stop there. Continue your plan right through the full 100 days. I have completed an Excel workbook to help you complete this critical exercise. If you would like a copy, please email *templates@westshore hospitalitygroup.com*.

Your 100-day plan is like a Gantt chart. It's broken down into weeks—so Week One, Week Two, and so on, all the way up to 100 days. Everything that is going to go into the chart and fill up these weeks is divided into four buckets:

- Goals
- People development
- Projects
- Meetings

The first section is goals. Here, I want you to think about what your goals are for your organization. Go back to concepts covered in this book: your vision statement and your rally cry. Put those down. Also put down the three core drivers or goals you decided on in your one-year plan. These are three goals you will be working *toward* during these 100 days; they may not be completed in the timeframe, but they will be active. Make sure you note when they are due.

The next section is people development. This whole book has been based on the concept of "you can't do it alone"—if you want to scale, you need to find the people to help you grow your organization. Investing in your people, therefore, is key. For these 100 days, map out your activities, interactions, and plans with regard to people development. These could be many things. You could, for example, implement a workshop teaching your people how to coach. It could be a workshop on a new skill, like financial management. There may be a new one-on-one strategy you're planning to implement between day seventy-five and day ninety. Put it all down.

The third section is projects. Here, list the critical projects you have coming up. You will already have three critical projects listed in your one-year plan; make sure you also enter them in this 100-day plan. If there are more, add them in here. For example, you may be launching a new delivery program, or you're looking at redesigning health and safety. Get these projects down in one place, with their due dates next to them.

100-DAY EXECUTION PLAN

GOAL	Week 1 Who/What	Week 2 Who/What	Week 3 Who/What	Week 4 Who/What	Week 5 Who/What	Week 6 Who/What	Week 7 Who/What	Week 8 Who/What
ACTIONS 1. 2. 3.								
PEOPLE DEVELOPMENT ACTIONS 1. 2. 3.								
PROJECT ACTIONS 1. 2. 3.								
MEETING ACTIONS 1. 2. 3.								

100-DAY EXECUTION PLAN | CONTINUED

GOAL	Week 9 Who/What	Week 10 Who/What	Week 11 Who/What	Week 12 Who/What	Week 13 Who/What	Week 14 Who/What	Week 15 Who/What
ACTIONS 1. 2. 3.							
PEOPLE DEVELOPMENT ACTIONS 1. 2. 3.							
PROJECT ACTIONS 1. 2. 3.							
MEETING ACTIONS 1. 2. 3.							

The last section is meetings. Chapter 9, "Communication and Meeting Rhythm" is helpful here. See which meetings you have upcoming in the next 100 days, and which ones you would like to make space for. Be detailed, so that your plan is as comprehensive as possible.

What we're trying to do here is map out everything you've currently committed to in the next 100 days. Our aim is to get you to look at these 100 days in one view, so that you have a zoomed-out, overall picture.

That's step one.

For step two, I want you to *priority* rank each of the activities you've written down in this plan. (I always say that my job as a coach usually isn't to convince people to take more action; it's to convince them to take less.) I know this feels like a hard task, but it's necessary. You want to make sure you have the time, capacity, and resources to make this plan a reality. That won't happen if you overcommit.

Step three is going through your list again and dividing them into "must-dos" and "should-dos." "Must-dos" are what we, as leaders, believe is most important *right now*. That might include the delivery of specific goals. Or it could be projects that have a tight timeframe and must be executed and delivered on. "Should-dos" are less urgent.

This step forces us to pay attention to what matters. Some of the "should-dos" on the list are going to be easier to complete than the "must-dos." They'll make us feel better, and so it's tempting to spend your time ticking them off rather than focusing on the more tangled "must-dos." Don't let that happen. Focus your time, attention, and resources on where your company needs them most.

This entire exercise of completing your 100-day plan, from step one to step three, may take up to two hours, but it is well worth the investment of your time. It helps everyone see what execution looks like for the whole team and shows them what needs to happen on a weekly basis. You can use it in your weekly meetings and one-on-ones to ensure you're staying on track, especially if you're trying to do something new. The goal is to get clear on what execution looks like, the priority of everything that goes along with that, and what success looks like.

You want to make sure you're seeing wins and progress—even if they're small—during this 100-day period. For example, if you want to reduce labor costs by 1.4 percent over the next year, the goal for the 100-day program might be to reduce it by 0.6 percent.

Be committed to the goal, be committed to the result—and be flexible on the approach. You know the destination you want to get to, but the vehicle might change. Periodically, determine whether what you're doing is producing the results. Course correct whenever necessary to achieve your goals.

YOUR VISION BOARD

The underlying concept of your 100-day plan and your execution-focused strategy is clarity. What people want in times of extreme challenge and change is clarity. Your people need *clarity* in what they should focus on, where to direct their efforts, and what matters most. A 100-day plan gives your team that focus. It directs their energies toward the key goals and achievements you've set for the year.

But clarity is also important for you as a leader. If you're going to steer this ship, then you need clarity of *vision*. You have to be absolutely clear about where you want to go and the results you want to achieve. Every single sports team, high-performing business team, and celebrity CEO—whether that's Elon Musk, Tim Cook, or Mark Cuban—have absolute clarity of vision of what they're looking to accomplish. And the way you capture that clarity is through a vision board.

Most people roll their eyes when I mention a vision board. They think I've watched too much of *The Secret*. (It's a video that came out ten years ago—if you haven't seen it, don't go back and watch it because it's very, very cheesy at this stage.) But the truth is that 80 percent of people are visual learners. And a vision board lets us attach pictures to our goals. It helps us see what we want to achieve in images, and so it makes those goals feel more real to us; we remember them better. I encourage my clients to make a personal vision board, a company vision board, and a team vision board. These help you move away from texts, P&L statements, and metrics to create rich and vivid visuals that connect us to the emotion and benefit of the achievement we're looking for.

It's simple to make a personal vision board: take a piece of paper and divide it into four quadrants. In the first top quadrant, focus on your professional life. What are you looking to achieve professionally for the year? Jot down any five to ten things. It could be opening a new restaurant, launching a new menu, achieving your bonus target—anything.

In the second quadrant, focus on your personal life. You want your personal goals to be side by side with your professional goals so that you can see how they connect and compare. What do you want to focus on in your personal life? Perhaps you want to go on vacation or spend more time with your kids. You could want to read more. List down any five to ten things. Make sure they're vivid goals you can imagine.

12-MONTH VISION BOARD | PERSONAL

PERSONAL

PROFESSIONAL

FRIENDS & FAMILY

COMMUNITY

MATT ROLFE

mattrolfe.com

WESTSHORE
ONLINE

The third quadrant deals with your goals for your family and friends. What do you want to achieve with your family? If you're single, what are the experiences you want to achieve with your friends? The purpose of this quadrant is to make sure we're not just focusing on our professional lives and ending up with no meaningful personal relationships.

Your last quadrant focuses on community. Inside of the restaurant community, how do you want to be seen? Who do you want to interact with? How are you working with COVID-19 recovery in the larger hospitality industry as a whole?

Remember that these quadrants are not equally weighted. You may have a lean community quadrant at this stage and very full personal quadrant. Or you could have a busy professional quadrant and not too many things you want to achieve personally in the coming year. Don't worry about it being unequally weighted. Aim for five to ten things, but make sure you're only noting down what you really want to do.

Once you have your lists, go to Google or Pinterest and search out vivid images for each of the bullets. Just have fun with this. Find images that are meaningful to you and that you care about. In my old vision board, I have an image of Michael Jordan hugging Phil Jackson in my professional quadrant. It's there to remind me to step back and be a coach. As a coach, I need to support those around me from the sidelines while they execute on the court. And since I made that, we've launched a coaching business that supports a lot of Michael Jordans out there to do incredible things. In my family quadrant, there's a picture of a young girl standing on a baseball diamond at third base and a young boy standing as shortstop. Just looking at that brings up such incredible emotion in me.

I have a four-year-old daughter now that I didn't have before. We struggled so much to get pregnant; we did have to go to fertility clinics. And as I write this, my wife is pregnant again, and we're hopeful for a healthy baby soon.

It feels like these opportunities manifested in my mind and then in my life, and by working toward them with full commitment, they became a reality. That's what a vision board should be for you. I want you to tape it up everywhere you can—everywhere you'll see it. I have one on my computer and on my phone, and I have a printout taped to my bathroom mirror. Program these wants and desires into your subconscious mind so that you're constantly looking for ways to work toward them as goals. Make them your reality.

Keep revisiting them. Every year when my Christmas tree goes up, I begin my vision board exercise again. Then there's a new one in place. I have one for myself, one for the team, and a common one for the family. It gives me the clarity I need to keep moving forward and make the life I truly want. I hope it does the same for you.

✂

KEY TAKEAWAYS

- Create a 100-day execution plan.

- The plan has four blocks: goals, people development, projects, and meetings.

- You must prioritize what's in the plan.

- Capture and share your vision with a vision board—most people learn visually.

CONCLUSION

We have been through quite a journey in this book, and I hope that you enjoyed it as much as my team and I did putting it together. I want to go back to where we started, to intent. It is great to read a book, it is great to consume content, and if you made it this far, I really do applaud you. If you made it this far, you are looking for something: looking for change, looking for a solution, or looking for a result for yourself, your team, or your business. Now it is time to be selfish, to be intentional, to be focused, and to make sure you get what you wanted from your time invested in this book.

The following pages summarize some of the critical points that we have covered. Review this list, circle the one to three lessons (to start) that, if you implemented or acted on them, would have the biggest impact on your business today. The difference between average leaders and great leaders is their ability to create clarity on the actions needed to move their team toward their goals. Now is your chance: get clear, get focused, and commit to taking massive action.

You now have all the strategies and steps to reach your goals. But remember: strategy creation is the easy part; execution is hard. In the same way, reading this book was the easy part, and implementing new plans in your business is the hard part. Commit to taking action.

We covered a ton of content that spanned over many areas. To summarize:

- The only way to engage and grow trust in a team is to start with vulnerability.
- A clear plan creates focus and momentum toward accomplishing your goals.
- Building your vision along with others who believe in it accelerates goal achievement.
- Assumptions don't create top performers.
- To achieve your goals, you must be in charge of your time and measure results around results-producing activities.
- People development happens by design. It's the foundation for top-performing teams and their success.
- Building a team of coaches creates a competitive point of difference that other organizations can't match.
- Communication often fails to make it through the company. To be successful, you must *over*communicate.
- Establish a clear, 100-day plan to keep the focus.

The only thing left to do now is to put your newfound knowledge into action. Though you are probably brimming with enthusiasm and ideas after finishing this book, don't try to implement everything at once. Pinpoint three things that will best help you achieve your desired results, and then get to work.

And remember: you can't do it alone. Share this book with your leadership team, execute the strategies, and join the online community. If you need extra help, please feel free to reach out at *info@ westshorehospitalitygroup.com*.

Put success in your calendar and execute!

ABOUT THE AUTHOR

Matt Rolfe is a coach, speaker, and entrepreneur who mentors the top 10 percent of the hospitality industry in unlocking their true potential. With a primary focus on personal development, Matt enables high-performing leaders to build unified teams and effectively delegate responsibilities for maximum growth. He is the founder of Results Hospitality and Westshore Hospitality Group, where he has worked with hundreds of leadership teams throughout North America. Beginning his career with companies like Bacardi and Labatt/Anheuser-Busch, Matt is an industry expert dedicated to helping leaders examine the human element of their business and execute effective team-building strategies unique to their needs. Matt lives in Toronto with his wife, Lindsay; their two children; and their golden retriever.

CPSIA information can be obtained
at www.ICGtesting.com
Printed in the USA
BVHW042353080822
643954BV00003BA/5